THE SILENCING OF BABYLON

A Spiritual Commentary on the Revelation of John

John Guimond, Capuchin

A powerful angel picked up
a stone like a huge millstone
and hurled it into the sea
and said:

"Babylon the great city
shall be cast down like this, with violence,
and nevermore be found!"

(Rev 18:21)

PAULIST PRESS
New York/Mahwah, N.J.

Library of Congress Cataloging-in-Publication Data

Guimond, John.
 The silencing of Babylon : a spiritual commentary on the Revelation of John / by John Guimond.
  p. cm.
 Includes bibliographical references.
 ISBN 0-8091-3239-7
 1. Bible. N.T. Revelation—Commentaries. I. Title.
BS2825.3.G78 1991
228'.07—dc20   91-3021
                        CIP

Published by Paulist Press
997 Macarthur Boulevard
Mahwah, New Jersey 07430

Printed and bound in the
United States of America

CONTENTS

FOREWORD

I have spent many beautiful hours studying, praying and sharing the message of the book of Revelation in scripture study groups. I have therefore developed a point of view that is in large measure my own, and I have uncovered in this beautiful though mysterious writing a powerful message for myself and for society. On the chance that this insight might prove useful to others and perhaps dispel some of the unreal and impractical applications that so often surface concerning this work, I have decided to put some of my reflections into writing, heeding in this way the words of Jesus to the seer: "Write what you now see" (Rev 1:11).

1

INTRODUCTION

Historically the book of Revelation is best situated in the reign of the Roman emperor Domitian (81–96 A.D.) who cleared his way to power through the assassination of his brother the emperor Titus (79–81 A.D.). One of the means this emperor used to consolidate his empire was the concept of emperor worship, something like honoring a country's flag but with deeper connotations. If a man is divine (as assumed in emperor worship), then that man ought to be followed without questioning. To the emerging Christian church, this could only be seen as blasphemy against Jesus Christ, the one and only divine man. Resistance on the part of the church led to what has been called the second general persecution of the church and the exile to the island of Patmos of a Christian leader who identifies himself to us as "John, your brother." Tradition has identified him with the apostle John, perhaps to give greater credibility to his powerful message.

Our impression might be that John wrote his whole book from the experience of a Sunday afternoon vision, but that is not really what he tells us. In his introduction he makes a statement that is important in understanding the creative movement of his work: "Write down . . . what you see now and will see in time to come" (1:19). From this we may infer that a long process of revelation has gone on in the writer's life which he has finally put into writing after it has sufficiently matured in his mind. There is a tendency to see the revelation of God in our life as a one-time experience, whereas it is really an ongoing process that spans our lifetime.

To write his book, John uses a process of code writing that we know as apocalyptic. The purpose of such a code is to comfort and instruct people under persecution without alerting the persecutors to what is really being said. The code, in apocalyptic writing, is numerical, scriptural and mythological. To take the images at their face value would be to badly misunderstand the intent of the author. Everything is symbolic of something else. Without proper background, one could hardly understand such a complex work as apocalypse.

Revelation relies heavily on such works as Daniel, Ezekiel, Joel, Genesis and no doubt many apocalyptic writings that have not found their way into the Bible. Of course, since its message is Christian, it will rely most of all on the Christian message which, for the author, will color his interpretation of the Jewish Bible. The number code John uses is hardly his own construction. It was already well established by the time he wrote his work. Three stands for emphasis and for the divine. In Revelation it will also stand for the opposite to the divine, the false trinity of the dragon, the beast and the false prophet. Four is the symbol for the world and five stands for ministry in the church. Both of these numbers are in evidence in, for instance, the writings of Deutero-Isaiah (Is 40–55). Seven is the complete number, courtesy of the book of Genesis (chapter 1, notably) and is used extensively in Revelation. Twelve stands for the twelve tribes of Israel and the twelve apostles of Jesus; hence it is a number that identifies the believing people, the Judeo-Christians. Multiply this number by its root and you have one hundred and forty-four thousand which stands for all the believing people in the history of Christianity. Six is just one number short of perfection and therefore represents the illusion that so often imitates the reality so closely as to fool people, the messages of worldly values that give the illusion of being sound, whereas, in the broad picture of what makes life truly successful, they are really flawed.

Another number will also surface in Revelation—three and a half years or its equivalent in months or weeks. This is a reminder of the three and a half years of persecution launched against the Jewish people by Antiochus Epiphanes (175–164 B.C.E.), the ominous and unstable Greek king of Syria (see 1 and 2 Maccabees). Since Antiochus sought to convince people of his own divinity, his career was reminiscent of that of the equally ominous Domitian.

The mythology is generally Middle Eastern and does not have much meaning to us at this point in history. The dragon, of course, is central to it, and he is found, under various names (Leviathan, Yam, Tiamat, etc.) in all the ancient religious myths of the region. The beast comes to us by courtesy of the book of Daniel, and the false prophet has a long history already evident in the clash between Hananiah and Jeremiah (Jer 27–28) and given a deeper identity in the apocalyptic sections of the synoptic gospels (Mk 13:22; Mt 24:24) and even more clearly in the letters of John (1 Jn 2:18, etc.) and Paul (2 Thes 2:3–12).

The structure of Revelation is disputed. My own insight which I offer in this book is that it is both cyclic and chiastic. For the untutored, cyclic refers to the grouping of seven symbols in Revelation that are repeated seven times (or six times according to some authors) to form a whole message. It is sometimes difficult for us to understand cyclic writing since each cycle tells us the whole story from one specific perspective. A modern example might be the writing of a biography from a series of perspectives. For instance, an author might write the whole history of my geographical movement: born in Detroit, raised in the province of Quebec, in military service in Germany, in ministry at several different locations, and finally death at a certain place. Next he might go into my educational experience, then the whole panorama of my faith life and so on. That would be cyclic writing in roughly the style of Revelation.

A chiastic structure was a popular way of arranging a work in ancient times. Such a structure is used extensively in the sacred writings of the New Testament: for instance, the great chiasmus of the passion of Christ in the gospel of Mark and the entire gospel of Matthew which is arranged in a chiastic order of seven parts. The writings of John are also chiastic in many parts. This structure allowed for orderly narration and cross-referencing of the work and no doubt served as a memory jog when books so often had to be memorized for presentation to the faithful due to the shortage of manuscripts. The chiastic structure in Revelation, as I understand it, goes like this:

        Seven Signs

Seven Trumpets   Seven Bowls

    Seven Seals   Seven Sights

Seven Letters   Seven Calls

Each of the divisions relates in some way to the opposite division. For instance, the letters and the calls are addressed to the church, the seals and the sights relate to the causes and resolutions of suffering in the world, the trumpets and the bowls speak of sin and its (often self-actuated) punishment. That leaves the central cycle of the signs which is the middle of the chiasmus and the core of the message. It outlines the cosmic struggle between good and evil, God and Satan, which is in progress in the world and in which we are all caught up by the very fact that we are human. When I can identify a chiastic structure in ancient writings, I can also identify what the author sees as most important since that will stand in the center. This is different from our modern concept of writing which builds up the suspense in a linear fashion, with the full development of the message being placed at the end of the book.

One of the most obvious elements of the book of Revelation is its use of contrasts. There is no light without a corresponding shadow, no holiness without a corresponding evil, no reality without a corresponding illusion. The list is long and new contrasts are uncovered at each reading. There is a Holy Trinity and an unholy trinity, a true resurrection and a false resurrection, an angel of light and an angel of darkness, two witnesses for God and two witnesses for the dragon, a holy mother and a prostitute, a holy city and a Babylon, a signing from God and a signing from Satan, a cup of God's wrath and a cup of lewdness, a sea of glass and a sea of chaos. One could go on for a long time in this listing of contrasts. The message, however, is clear: it takes a lot of insight to distinguish between reality and illusion, between truth and the misleading half-truth. As John tells us, "a certain wisdom is needed here" (13:18) or we will take the illusion for the reality, the lie for the truth, the blasphemous name for the divine name.

That is John's purpose: to give us enough wisdom so we will not be fooled by the honeyed enticements of worldliness and self-centered living. The mark of the beast, to John, is very simple—it is greed in all its forms. The mark of God is also clear—it is selfless dedication to the service of the Lamb and a loving surrender to the judgment of God in our life.

John's purpose in writing his book is not just to comfort his persecuted church but, above all, to give us a sound tool for discernment. That tool is as valid today as it was two thousand years ago and, if we learn how to use it properly, it will enrich our lives and steer us clear of dead-end choices. Hence, for me, the importance of this book is not in what it reveals of the future but in what it reveals of my life right now. The struggle that he outlines is played out not only on the world's stage but on the stage of my own heart.

My reflections on the book of Revelation are not meant to be an exegetical explanation of that book. That has been done before and done very well. My wish is to draw from this beautiful book a spiritual message that is applicable to myself and to others, hopefully without doing violence to the original intent of the author. If scripture is to have meaning for us, it must be applied to our needs and our lives. The word of God is not so much meant to be studied as to be prayed and lived. If we keep our interest solely on what the message was to the readers of two thousand years ago, we may uncover very little relevance for the readers of today. The power of scripture is that it bridges history and, like the two-edged sword, cuts into our heart and the depths of our very being. That I know what it says is important; that I know what it says to me personally is vital. Scripture is not a weapon that I use to uncover the rascals in the world, it is the tool that I use to uncover the rascal dwelling within my own heart. If the message that I draw from the word is not applicable to me, perhaps I have not read it with enough humility and openness of heart.

Revelation, to be read fruitfully, should not be looked upon as the unfolding of history but as a call to enhance the quality of our Christian life. The clue to that is the cycle of the churches which is not only a pat on the back for the Christians but, as often, a slap on the hand. The struggle is my struggle and the dragon is fighting the Lamb in the very recesses of my being. Christians are not an elite beyond the struggle but active participants in the midst of it. For me to use the book to judge the world is to miss the point. The judgment is above all a judgment on myself, on my attitudes, on the lies that I have made my own or that I am tempted to buy into. Let us look, then, at how we may approach this great work and draw from it the benefits promised us by the seer: "I will make the victor a pillar in the temple of my God" (3:12).

To approach a serious study of the book of Revelation, I need first of all to be fairly familiar with the other books of the Bible from which Revelation draws extensively in the shaping of its message. If I do not know something about the passages that the book refers to, I will not know what the author is trying to say to me. Since Revelation is a highly structured work, I need to be somewhat familiar with its literary plan. The chiastic structure, as I have said, is for the purpose of clarity and of cross-reference. Opposite cycles throw light on each other and may profitably be read together. Since each cycle outlines a perspective of life, each cycle also needs to be understood as a unit. One will quickly note that each of the seven cycles ends with an account of the end of the world: 3:21, 6:12–17, 11:15–19, 14:14–20, 16:17–21, 20:11–15, 22:12–20. One may easily deduce that the author did not mean to infer that the world would end seven times but, rather, that each of his meditations brought him to that final drama toward which all of history is headed and which will put an eternal seal, of triumph or of defeat, on our humanity.

Revelation, like a fine wine, is best sipped slowly rather than gulped down at one swallow. A preliminary reading of the whole book is advisable to get a flavor of its style and message, but any serious study must concentrate thoroughly on the message of each cycle. As we become more and more familiar with the style and the message of the book, its meaning will deepen for us and its usefulness as a tool for self-study will be enhanced. We will also begin to make more and more connections with the rest of scripture and we will be thrilled to notice how well it fits in with the overall message of the Bible. As we remember Eve and the serpent, we will recall the holy mother and the dragon; as we read about the ideal holy city in Ezekiel, we will think of the ideal holy city in Revelation; as we reflect on the majesty of Christ in Ephesians, we will be led back to the sevenfold majesty of the King of kings in Revelation 19:11–16.

The praise prayers in the book of Revelation are among the most magnificent in the New Testament. To study the great trinitarian hymn of Revelation 15 is to desire to make it part of our own prayer life. The hymn of the triumph of the elect in chapter 12 is one of the most powerful teachings on discernment that I have found in the Bible. One could go on and on, awed at the beauty and the wisdom of the book, or one could bog down on the grim visions it unfolds and turn away with a shudder. All depends on our perspective in reading. Therefore, to read Revelation properly is a must if we would read it at all. Otherwise, we may get lost in the sea of chaos and never quite make it to the sea of crystal on which floats the eternal temple of God.

My method for sharing my reflections on Revelation is simple and, I hope, will make the reader's study of the book easier and more meaningful. The book is divided into seven cycles to which are added two stage-settings. Each cycle, except for the first and the last, includes a couple of pauses after the sixth cycle to reflect on some heavenly vision—what I am fond of referring to as the coffee breaks. This simple division of the book has been maintained in my reflections, and each paragraph that I will be commenting on will be noted so you can refer to it easily in your Bible. My reflections are my own, born of the many hours of study that I have consecrated to this book. I hope they will provide practical applications of the text for you. The message is not rose water; it is powerful and sometimes disquieting, but that is the flavor of life, and scripture addresses the deep realities of life, not the pie-in-the-sky pietism of the "one of these days." The Bible translation that I will be working with is the New American Bible.

At the beginning of each division of Revelation, I will give you a brief overview of that division and a thought on how it fits into the overall message. My intent is to avoid over-explaining and thus robbing you of the chance to make your own discoveries. Scripture does not present an "only-this-and-nothing-more" message. It is dynamic and will unfold an ongoing message for you that will change and deepen depending on where you are at in your own life. The word speaks to life and life speaks to the word. If it were not so, we would be following the dead letter of the law rather than the covenant of the heart which promises that "all from least to greatest shall know me" (Jer 31:34). The emphasis here is on "me," and that speaks of a relationship rather than a document. To know the Lord requires dialogue, and dialogue can never be static.

It is my sincere wish that this book may provide you with "an open door" (3:8) to Revelation through which you may enter at your leisure to be refreshed, renewed and challenged by the ever-present vitality of the word of God.

A BREAKDOWN OF THE CHIASMUS OF REVELATION

Introduction—The divine author and the human author—proper credentials for Christian proclamation chapter 1

1. **Letters to the Seven Churches.**
   Advice and warning to Christian communities.
   Looking at our attitudes toward church.
   Chapters 2 and 3.

2. A preparation:
   The heavenly setting.
   Who it is who directs our human destiny.
   The Seven Seals.
   Reflection on human suffering.
   Chapters 4 through 7.

3. **The Seven Trumpets.**
   Judgment on human sin.
   What causes the deepest pain in our life.
   Chapters 8 through 11.

4. **The Seven Signs**
   The center of the ideological struggle.
   Life and the imitation of life.
   The world situation that brings forth sin.
   Chapters 12 through 15.

5. **The Seven Bowls.**
   The consequences of our sins:
   on others.
   on nature itself.
   The cosmic aspect of sin
   Chapter 16.

6. **The Seven Sights.**
   Challenging the sin-situation.
   How to remedy the evil.
   Inevitable triumph of God's plan in the world.
   Chapters 17 through 20.

7. **The Seven Calls.**
   The ideal we strive to present to the world.
   Criteria for church membership.
   Return to the Lord's presence.
   Chapters 21 and 22.

2

THE EARTHLY SETTING: REVELATION 1

As we begin the book of Revelation, we are introduced to the purpose for its writing and we are given an extensive look at the credentials of its authors, both divine and human. There is a special purpose in that. Looking at the divine credentials builds up our love and trust in God, the author of the book. It places us on that level of ecstasy—of awed consideration of the divine—that brings us to a contemplation of heaven, our goal and the reason for our Christian life. We are left with a clear image of who God is and why it is expedient for us to put our trust in him.

The second purpose for this section flows naturally from the first. It is the credentials of the prophet, what is required of us if we are to reflect the message of the Lord to the world. The flavor of Christian ministry is outlined for us. Having looked at the ideal, we will be given a look at how it is carried out, or not carried out, in the church.

The last section of the introductory chapter is a reflection on the prophet's own dialogue with Jesus—how he sees his Lord and how he understands the calling of his Lord in his life. Once we have become convinced of the credibility of both the prophet and the prophet's Lord, we are ready to enter into the message of the book of Revelation and to enter into it with serene confidence. Our Lord has been explicit in his message: "There is nothing to fear."

PART 1—THE CREDENTIALS OF THE AUTHOR

1:1–3

There is a beatitude at the beginning of the book of Revelation and there is another beatitude at the end (22:14) and five other beatitudes in between for a total of seven, the number in Revelation that speaks of fullness. We can too easily get caught up in the bad news of the book and forget that it is the good news that is really emphasized, the news that God is in charge and that his will is going to triumph over all obstacles and all persecutions. At the outset we are invited to place ourselves on the side of God so we will be part of his assured victory and its eternal celebration.

The first beatitude of Revelation relates to our ability to read and understand the will of God for humanity and to our willingness to act on what has been learned. Simply to hear the word and not do anything about it is rather futile. There is little point in learning anything if the learning does not influence our actions. There is in us a strong tendency to leave a wide gap between what we know and how we act, and the possible reason for that is that one learns with the brain but the feelings and convictions most often determine our actions. If our learning does not somehow sink down to the level of our feelings, it has very little impact on our lives. The beatitude, therefore, has to do with both hearing and heeding—acting upon what has been heard.

The appointed time is near. Two thousand years of history must not blind us to the fact that, for us, the time is as near as our death. No one is given more than a lifetime in this world and no one is promised a specific number of years for that lifetime. No matter what my age is, the time is near, and if I am not careful to live according to the will of God, death may find my life's task unfulfilled and my spiritual growth arrested.

All of us must bear witness to the word of God and to the testimony of Jesus in our life. Words are not enough because we learn from Revelation that witnessing comes mostly from symbolic actions. If the actions of our life are not witnesses to the word of God, any preaching we do, any discussion we engage in, will be completely futile. It is not words that convince but a life lived according to the eternal word.

1:4-8

In a very few words John gives us the whole reality of God. He uses the very Jewish "number game" to do so. The message he receives is given by three personalities—God, the spirits, and Jesus. God has three attributes as does Jesus. And there are seven spirits, the fullness of wisdom and power.

The three attributes of God have a powerful impact on my life. He is he who is. God is part of my life right now; he is the full reality of my life. He is he who was; God has been part of everything that has ever happened to me. All my history can be explained in God's will for me. He is he who is to come; God will take care of my future. Nothing will ever happen to me apart from what God has decreed should happen. I can trust God to bring me to fullness of life.

The three attributes of Jesus are also breathtaking. He is the faithful witness. He tells us everything that God has sent him to tell; he holds back nothing. All that we need to know about God has been revealed to us by Jesus. He is the first-born from the dead; he has inaugurated a new way of living, an eternal way. If we are the brothers and the sisters of Jesus, then we also shall be born to this eternal life since "first-born" implies that other births will follow. And Jesus is the ruler of the kings of the earth. He is the powerful one who leads the destiny of all others. No one can contradict him. No one can give a witness other than the witness he has given. We have in these three attributes the full reality of Jesus: he is truth, he is fullness of life, he is power.

However, the revelation of God is not complete in this tremendous greeting. The paragraph ends with another revelation of God from a slightly different perspective. Again God reveals three attributes of himself. He is the Alpha and the Omega, he is the One who is, who was, and who is to come, and he is the Almighty.

The Alpha and the Omega represent all the alphabet, and therefore all of reality, because everything we can name is contained in the alphabet and all the alphabet is contained in God. The second attribute has already been encountered but may be seen here in a different context. God is he who is, was, and will come; that is, he is all of history and nothing that can possibly happen can happen outside of God. If he is all of history, then he controls all of history and his cause will—must!—triumph. And God is the Almighty; he is the fullness of power, he is all the potential of life and everything that can be imagined. If all that can be imagined (the Alpha to Omega) is contained in God, then all I can imagine has a potential for life, for being, and that makes me one with my creator at the very source of his essence, creativity.

Having received this revelation of who God is, we can only quiet our mind and heart and listen to his voice. He will tell us everything that we need to know for our happiness and our salvation.

1:9–11

Having received a revelation of divinity, we are now brought to earth to listen to the calling of the prophet. As we have heard the credentials of God, so now we hear the credentials of his servant.

He is a brother to the people he writes to. He is not their father, their master, or one with any title of superiority, but a brother, an equal who shares as an equal. A prophet must never lord it over the people to whom he prophesies. If he cannot be their brother, he has no valid message for them.

Not only is the prophet a brother to the people but he shares a common ideal with them. He shares the distress—all the problems of life, all the sufferings and frustrations, all the temptations of the rest of humanity. He shares the kingly reign; he is part of the church, a member of the faith community to which he writes. It is only those who are within the church who have a right to critique the church. And he shares the endurance; like them, he has placed his hopes in the future and he has accepted the reality that fullness of happiness is not to be found in this world.

Another thing that makes the prophet a credible witness is that he is persecuted for the faith. He has not put human respect above his spiritual convictions; he is willing to endure any persecution that may come to him as a result of his beliefs. Since he is one with his people, since he shares their faith and is willing to accept persecution for that faith, the prophet is ready and able to speak for the Lord to his people. There is no self-glory, no greed and no cowardice in him. He, like Jesus, will be a faithful witness.

1:12–16

John gives us a cosmic image of Jesus. Wool comes from the animal kingdom, fire and water are elements of life, brass is a mineral, and the sun and stars are heavenly bodies. Jesus, in his person, encompasses all of creation. He is "the First and the Last," the one in whom everything else has its being.

The fact that Jesus has the two-edged sword, the power to destroy those who will not accept him, should give great consolation to the seer who is in exile precisely because there are people who have rejected the lordship of Jesus. As the two-edged sword gives Jesus power over the world, so do the seven stars he holds give him power over all spiritual beings, and his presence among the seven lampstands reminds us that he also has full power in his church. Already we have a glimpse of the eventual victory of Jesus over all the forces of this world and of the next and over all the negative elements in his church.

1:17–18

The challenge of Jesus in my life is a death-resurrection challenge. As I catch sight of him, I am challenged to let go of many things, to "fall down as though dead" so that he may raise me up again to a greater life. There is indeed nothing to fear—not from persecution, not from death, not from God. Jesus has gone through the whole cycle; he has died and now lives so that he can lead me safely to my eternal haven. Jesus holds the keys of death and the nether world, the two ultimate negatives that can lead me to fear. If I live in and with Jesus, nothing can betray me into those two horrors because no one can open its doors except Jesus himself, and he is on my side. What an encouragement there is in this to make Jesus the Lord of my life!

1:19–20

"What you have seen, and what is happening, and what will happen afterwards." Revelation is an ongoing thing; it is never finished as long as we live. Just as we receive constantly, so must we "write" constantly, share with one another the revelation we receive, and never stop sharing it. The Lord makes no revelation that is strictly for me alone. All revelation is meant to be shared, to be eventually divulged. "What you have whispered in locked rooms will be proclaimed from the rooftops" (Lk 12:3).

The more I discover the glory of Jesus in my life, the more eager I will be to share him with others. Although I must always respect the freedom of other people, I must not forget that the two-edged sword is poised against all who choose not to believe, not to accept the Lord. I am a witness, not just with words but with the way I live my life. Therefore, if my life does not make others eager to believe in Jesus, I cannot easily exonerate myself from blame. The sword, it must always be remembered, has two edges, and one of those edges is poised against the witnesses who do not live in a manner worthy of their heaven-appointed task.

3

FIRST CYCLE— THE LETTERS TO THE CHURCHES: REVELATION 2 AND 3

We now enter into the body of the book and we begin our journey with an assessment of the church community, its accomplishments and its failures, its goals and its obstacles. There are seven churches, a fact that is important on two levels. First of all, the seven cities mentioned are part of what we may call a mail route. The distance between each of them is that which a runner would cover in one day's work as he distributed the communications entrusted to him for the different communities. The runner, here, would reach a different city every day and so his tour of duty would take seven days, a full week, following which he could begin again in reverse order. Like the Christian prophet, he is on a constant tour of duty, bringing the message of the Lord to the world and facilitating charitable communications between all of its various communities.

Theologically, seven is also the complete number and so speaks of a message intended for all the Christian people of all places and of all times. The message is for us, the criticism is for us, and so are the promises. It is easy for us to see reflected in our own communities some of the problems, the accomplishments and the failings of these seven town-communities of what is now modern Turkey.

In this first cycle, there is a call for us to assess where we are at and what we hope to accomplish. It is our own examination of conscience before we are allowed to enter into the sacred ground of God's eternal home where "nothing unclean will enter" (21:27).

PART 2—FIRST CYCLE: THE CHURCHES

2:1-7

With all the cleverness of the church of Ephesus in recognizing phonies, it had still "turned aside from its early love," and it ran the risk of itself becoming a phony that preached a way of love which it did not fully exemplify. It is a warning that all Christians need to take to heart as they face their task of evangelization throughout the world. Perhaps our lack of success in converting the world stems from the fact that we, as a church, have also turned aside from our early fervor, that fervor which turned the mighty Roman empire into a Christian state. It is not hard to become convinced of that when we consider how the early Christians lived and how we, by comparison, now live. There is little about the Christian nations to make them attractive to the rest of the world. When the developing countries think of Christian states, what comes to their mind but imperialism, disunity and the oppression of weaker nations? How have we failed to be converted by the message of conversion that we are called to bring to others? Like the Nicolaitans of old, those who bear the name of Christians these days very often give little honor to Christianity.

The question needs to become even more personal. How have I fallen from my first fervor? How have I watered down the ideals that once moved me to conversion? That is where, ultimately, the question must rest. Knowing what I resolved to become, knowing the ideals that motivated me, how far have I gone in the living out of my Christianity? To criticize the Christians out there is of little value if the Christian within is not all that he has been called to be. I will convert no one until I have converted myself.

What do I need to do to deserve being fed from the tree of life, the tree from which Adam and Eve were denied a share? I must go back to re-examine the days of my early fervor and see what ideals I have watered down, what goals have become hazy, what compromises have seeped into my life. Then, obviously, I must return to my early fervor without returning to the unrealistic ideals that I held then, the ideals which, when they were challenged by my maturing understanding, were the occasion of a fall from my first fervor. To retain the good while removing the clutter can be a monumental task as we undergo the necessary purification that must follow any conversion experience. All the more difficult is the task when we consider that there is always the enemy voice to whisper to us that we should also remove some of the ideals in order to make for ourselves a more comfortable life.

2:8–11

Smyrna receives the shortest message because the Lord has nothing to reproach them for. Those closest to God are often those who receive the fewest communications from him. God speaks to those who need him the most, and God grants the most special favors to those who need those special favors in order to continue on in his service. To hear little from God is not necessarily a negative sign; it can be rather a proof of greater predilection. Those who need signs and wonders in order to believe are weak in faith. We tend too easily to think of a spiritual favor as a sign of one's worth, whereas it is far more likely to be a sign of one's weakness.

In one of those scriptural paradoxes that we so often encounter in the Bible, life can be death and death can be life. It is all a matter of who is Lord of my life. If my Lord is worldly interests, then I am fated to die since this world must die. If my Lord is God, then I am fated to live because God never dies. Physical death is a starting point, not an end. The real death is to be condemned to an eternity without God. Compared to that, all the comforts of this life are so much straw waiting to be burned. There are far better things on which to base my life than that.

The devil, who is lord of the second death—that is, of eternal damnation—has a special rage toward those who are faithful to the Lord. One of his more subtle persecutions is to attack their self-image. More will be written in Revelation about this "accuser" who seeks to cast us into the prison of self-blame and guilt feelings. The more we rely on God, the shorter and less effective his attacks will be. In this life, however, we will never be completely free of them. All of us will have to undergo our "ten days" of self-recrimination. Perhaps there is no other way to attain to the fullness of true humility which is to place all our reliance on God, the creator and therefore the affirmer of our life.

2:12-17

The sin of Pergamum was compromise—trying to get along as comfortably as possible in an un-Christian world. It is easy to fall into the sin of Pergamum—to compromise with un-Christian opinions, to enjoy un-Christian entertainment, to share in the comforts of our modern age even when these get in the way of properly serving God. Long gone are the days of the desert fathers when the ways of the world were completely and permanently given up for the sake of Christ! Nowadays we give a little and take back a little and wonder why we are not really progressing in our spiritual life.

We live in a dangerous social milieu. It is not violence that endangers us but the softness and amoral character of the life our civilization offers. Perhaps it is time, once again, to make a definitive break with the culture, to return to the desert, there to be fed not by the deceptions of our over-indulgent world but by the manna of God's word. It is noteworthy that the manna is "hidden." We cannot find it as long as we remain caught up in worldliness; it will be ours only if we also become "hidden," people who reserve themselves for something better than the indulgence, the half-truths and the subtle violence of our own age.

How can we know what our name really is when we let the world tell us who we are rather than taking the time and the effort to ask God? There is no short-cut; our name is learned in prayer and fasting, in self-denial, in taking on a different set of values than that offered by the world. To be named by the world is to be condemned to shallowness and slavery. Only God knows who I really am. Only God can reveal to me my inner being. The Nicolaitans of this world have nothing to give me but compromise and the agony of a lost identity.

2:18-29

The sin of Thyatira was the toleration of evil. The concept of "live and let live" does not find ready acceptance in the theology of the visionary John, and perhaps it should find a less ready acceptance in the rest of us. The problem is what to do about the evil that is around or, as seems the case here, Christian complacency and compromise. Sometimes the answer is even less Christian than the sin. "Ruling with a rod of iron" may make for good order but it is hardly compatible with charity. And not much better can be said for "shattering like crockery."

About the only person I can dare "rule with a rod of iron" is myself. Complacency is best eradicated at home. Then, perhaps, it will be less prominent in others. Nothing beats example for bringing people to a change of heart. When the discipline is directed outward, it can only be seen as interference or even repression.

Why then would Jesus make such a suggestion? Perhaps he is trying to emphasize the great harm done to the church by the lukewarm and compromising Christians. If the church is the leaven meant to transform the whole world, can it afford to be the wrong kind of leaven? If it is meant to be the salt of the earth, can it afford to lose its flavor? When all we are interested in is numbers, how can we retain quality? If we demanded more of Christians, perhaps Christianity could do more for the world. The practice of feeding Christians baby food, so to speak, means that Christians remain babies—self-centered, indulgent, and little better in the long run than the pagans we are called to bring to the faith. Perhaps, after all, a bit of iron would not be all that undesirable when it comes to dealing out church discipline. Lukewarm demands draw only lukewarm people while the enthusiastic and the self-disciplined go off in search of other causes and other faiths in the service of which they can better expend their energy.

The prophetess against whom John writes seems to feel that the best way to keep people in the church is to give them what they want. There is, I suppose, a spiritual equivalent to bread and circuses. When our aim is to please, we are not likely to make ethical demands on people. We will look the other way when breaches of ethics are evident for fear of losing people if we criticize their private sins. Always we are caught between the pastoral call to be gentle, forgiving and affirming and the prophetic call to demand justice and integrity. Perhaps the pastoral people (exemplified by the prophetess) and the prophetic people (like John) would do better to dialogue and learn from each other rather than take on opposite positions and accusatory tones that only deepen the chasms of misunderstanding. Both sides have a message, both sides are needed in the church, and neither side is complete without the other. When opinions become more important than cooperation, we may resort to the seduction of people and the increase of confusion in the church of Christ.

Arguments and accusations are of little value in the long run. Faith needs to be lived on a deeper level. The morning star—the sign of resurrection— will only be given to those who have truly died to themselves for the sake of Christ.

3:1–6

"I have not found your works complete in the sight of my God." A harsh message for Sardis. There is no praise for the people who choose to sit on their hands because they know the price of rocking the boat and they are not about to do that. They have the reputation of being alive—they do all the right things; they worship properly, they live in mutual love, they are honest—but they are dead, as anyone is dead who refuses to grow. In their concern not to anger the pagans by making converts, they are content to remain within their in-group and they make no room for newcomers. That, at least, is my reconstruction of the malady of Sardis. It is not such a strange sickness nor is it unique to that one people.

This fear of rocking the boat, of making people angry, of being criticized, keeps a lot of us from giving as fruitful a witness as we feel the call to. The main problem here is that, when we are too cautious, we quickly lose our enthusiasm, we fall asleep on our faith, we begin not to look too closely at life lest we see needs we are not desirous of doing anything about. To choose to take no risk is to choose to stagnate, to fall asleep.

The second problem we can get into when we want to avoid challenges is that of boredom with its inevitable cortege of sinful habits. As the people of Sardis fall more and more asleep in their complacency, they also begin to fray their moral fiber, they soil the white robe of their Christianity. With all their reputation for clean living, they are becoming a weight on the evangelical church and they are setting the foundation for serious moral problems.

All of us can take to heart the statement to the Sardis church: "The sum of your deeds is less than complete in the sight of God." We are called to a specific task that should involve all the moments of our life. Timidity means that something will not get done that we were called to do. We have not completed our task until we come to eternal life. We cannot rest on the memory of past triumphs. If we do so, we will be living in a museum. There is no life in a museum, only memories that give a warm glow and no challenge.

How can our name be in the book of the living if our life is dead weight? If we refuse to grow, to take chances, to forge ahead, to work creatively at the task assigned to us by our Lord, we are not really living and what right have we to hope that we will be seen as part of the living church? The statement, "Stand up and be counted," illustrates our need to be actively in the service of God and to boldly labor on the cutting edge of life. To really live, we must live intensely.

3:7–13

When one is ready, the Lord promises an open door—the opportunity to work in his service. No one can close that door because, if opportunity is lost in one direction, it is found in another. The hardest thing, I believe, is to wait until we are ready, until our work of inner growth warrants our being called to ministry. We always want to force open the door before the Lord is ready to open it to us, and thus our attempts at ministry can often become failures that lead us to discouragement.

How does one know when one is ready? I suppose the only way to know is to have stood fast in the way that our Lord has traced for us. Faithfulness is what opens wide the door for us. And faithfulness takes years of hanging on when very little result seems discernible. That is undeniably the hard part—to hold fast even when no success can be evidenced.

Why the importance of faithfulness? Perhaps because the

Lord wants us to be pillars. It is easy enough to be firebrands, to set about challenging and upsetting people, but to be pillars takes a lot of patience and a lot of reliability. As there must undoubtedly be firebrands, so must there be pillars—people who will always be there for others when they are needed, people of the kind that Saint Joseph was, people who are just.

The people of Philadelphia received the name of God—they are his people—the name of the city of God—they are its citizens—and the name of Jesus—they are his witnesses. Jesus' name is a new name, not what has always been done before but a new way, a new door opening to a new opportunity, a new solution to the problems of the world. The Christian stands before the world with a great dignity, a great gift and a great opportunity for service. These precious benefits must not be wasted.

3:14–22

Here again we have a triple title for Jesus. He is the Amen, that is the final end of all things. Jesus controls the eventual destiny of humankind; he is its final judge and will decide who will enter the kingdom and who will not. Jesus is the faithful Witness and true. All that he reveals to us is the truth and he reveals to us all the truth that we can understand. And Jesus is the Source of God's creation. What a tremendous title that is! All that was created was created in Jesus and therefore, in a most profound way, he is the new, the perfect Adam of whom we are all descendants. In that short phrase, the seer gives us a backward glance at Jesus, starting with the end and ending with the beginning.

Jesus invites the people of Laodicea to ask three things of him who has just identified himself by a triple title: gold refined by fire (good works done in spite of persecution), a white garment (a life dedicated to purity of living), and eye ointment so they can see clearly to follow the Lord and to accept his truth. It is interesting that the Laodiceans lacked in the spiritual order those very things with which they were rich in the physical order. If we cater to our physical life, we very often neglect our spiritual life. We need to choose which is the most important to us.

Jesus knocks at the door of our life, but only we can let him in; he will not force himself on us. It is not because Jesus can't come in unless we let him in since we know from the letter to the Philadelphians that he has the key; no door is locked to him. Yet there is no point in his forcing his way into our life if we do not want him, if we are satisfied with our physical wealth, because we would not make proper use of his grace; we would not partake in a life-giving way of the meal he provides.

The reward that Jesus offers us for letting him in, for warming up to his presence and spending our time with him, is a share in his own power, a place with him on his very throne. By following Jesus, we also become the Amen, we choose our eternal destiny in heaven, we become the faithful witness, we learn from him and therefore we know and we speak the truth, and we become the source of creation because, through our faithfulness, others will come to life and find salvation; we become new Adams, new Eves, to a multitude of people who will follow us. Can a greater destiny ever be offered to mere human beings by God than to share in the very attributes of the divinity? Woe to those who, after such beautiful promises, remain lukewarm!

THE HEAVENLY SETTING: REVELATION 4 AND 5

Having looked at the earthly setting of the message, we now look at its heavenly setting from which the drama outlined in Revelation will be directed. It is a reminder to us that our destiny is directed from heaven and there is no cause for fear or for frustration (5:4). Just because, from our narrow perspective, we don't understand God's direction of human history does not mean that it is not being directed properly.

Central to this section is the thought that Jesus is the one who makes sense out of life for us. Having gone through the human experience, he understands it perfectly and knows what we are going through. He is our safe refuge in the struggles of life.

Anchored in our firm hope in heaven and our full confidence in the power and the wisdom of our leader, we can now go on to examine the reality of life—its sufferings, its failures, its struggles, the flux of its ups and downs, its victories and defeats. Nothing can ever overcome us if we remain grounded in our Lord Jesus, the Lamb who is truly worthy of all trust.

PART 3—THE HEAVENLY SETTING

4:1-3

With imagery taken from the Old Testament, John introduces us to the divinity. The first truth he reveals to us is that we have a standing invitation to come to God; the door to heaven is open and we only have to climb up. In fact, we are urged to climb up in order to receive a fuller understanding of what our life is all about, of what destiny we have been prepared for. How do we climb? Through ecstasy—that is, through a stance of prayer and love of God and the willingness to spend time in his presence.

Prayer brings us before the awesome sparkle of God, before the joyful light of his countenance. We find the rainbow there, the timely reminder that God is faithful and that he will keep his word to us and deliver us from the waters of chaos, the bewildering situation of suffering and of injustice that we find ourselves immersed in as we live our life in this world.

4:4-8

Twenty-four elders, the representatives of the Jewish church (twelve tribes) and the Christian church (twelve apostles), surround the throne of God. Later on, we will be introduced to all the Christian believers (the one hundred and forty-four thousand), but for now these leaders are shown to us in a resplendence that is only a pale reflection of the splendor of God.

We also find a second group before the throne, and these are the seven spirits of God, representatives of his fullness of wisdom and of knowledge. The floor around the throne is a sea of glass. There is a transparence in God; he does not choose to hide from us but rather stands revealed for those who have taken a stance of prayerful ecstasy before him.

Another group is also introduced at this point—the four living creatures. Since four is the symbolic number for the whole world, these four creatures have a worldwide mission of proclamation. Their message is for everyone, not just for the church. Who are these mysterious beings in the guise of cherubim? The first thought that comes to mind is the four evangelists of whom these four beings have become the symbols. The evangelists have in fact put forth a message meant to be shared by the whole world. The good news of God's love and salvation is for everyone, not just for the members of the Christian church. Clearly, these four have a never-ending task of praising God and calling the church to an answering praise.

The number three is in evidence in the praise of the four living creatures. Three times they shout "Holy"; God has perfect holiness. They have three titles for the One on the throne; he is Lord (he has dominion over all the earth), he is God (the eternally perfect being) and he is almighty (he has the fullness of power). Finally, they extol the God of all history, he who was, who is, and who is to come. In God is a reality that has always been, that is now, that will always be.

4:9–11

At the call of the four living creatures, the noble leaders of the believing people intone their own song of praise to God. Because the ever-living God is the creator of the world, it is fitting that the world should praise him through the church. Continuing the symbol of the number three, the elders declare God worthy of receiving three kinds of worship. He is to be given glory because, as creator, he is the powerful One; he is to be given honor because God is the all-holy One; he is to be given praise because all of God's deeds are infinitely good. In creating the world, God did not make any mistakes; he created all things infinitely well, and we who are at the apex of that creation have the most urgent need to lead all the world into a hymn of praise to God. Indeed, how can we do any less and not demean the importance of our destiny?

Clearly, the main task of humanity and also its most precious privilege is to worship God and his Son Jesus. There is for us no more sacred duty than this—to come in adoration before the divinity where alone we find the sense, the meaning and the dignity of our life.

5:1–5

"I wept bitterly." As the seer is faced with the scroll of human history in which is found the solution to all the problems that plague humankind, he experiences the frustration of realizing that no one can open it, no one can make sense out of life for him. This is a familiar frustration for all of us as we struggle through life, wondering why it is so hard, why we are so often unhappy, why there is so much pain and so much wickedness. To know that the answer is there, just beyond our reach, only adds to our impatience to find out.

The angel calls out: "Who can open the scroll?" And the answer comes from the elder, the representative of the church, the one entrusted with the spreading of the good news of Christianity: the Lion who is a Lamb, the living One who has been slain, the one who is the fulfillment of past promises and the hope of future glory—that is the one who can open the scroll. Why? Because he has gone through the full cycle of the human experience; he has been born, has died, has resurrected and has returned to heaven from where he came. He knows from personal experience what a human life is all about. The only thing that will make sense out of our life for us is to have come to its eternal completion. Until that day we will remain enmeshed in the mystery, surrounded by all the anxious questions of suffering and sin for which, in this life, there is no answer unless we seek that answer in the Lord Jesus himself, the one—the only one—who really knows.

5:6–10

The seven eyes of the Lamb see all the places of the earth, a reminder of the Lamb's power to make sense out of our history. He has the vision from the mountaintop whereas we have the vision from the valley. He who has fullness of vision also has fullness of power—the seven horns. Not only can he make sense out of our world but he can lead it in the ways it needs to go to accomplish the task for which it has been created by God. Often we have a sense of aimlessness, of things going from bad to worse in spite of our efforts to remedy the situation. It is good to remember that, even though we may not be aware of it, God is accomplishing his will in the world. Moreover, the more we surrender ourselves to God's service, the better he can use us in the accomplishment of that will. We cannot afford to forget the fact that we are part of a great destiny, of a cosmic adventure, of an exodus experience meant to shape us into the eternal people of God.

The aromatic spices are an interesting symbol, a reminder to us that the prayers of the just are indeed a sweet fragrance to God and they have the power to bring down his blessings on the earth. God, in his infinite design, has chosen not to do it without us but rather to trust us to do our share in the work of the world's salvation. If we lag behind, the work lags behind, if we work with zeal and enthusiasm, the work advances. We determine how long it will take, but the outcome, eventually, will be that which God has chosen it to be. He is in charge. The One who reigns at the center of our heart can direct our life to the accomplishment of his will, and he can do so without doing violence to our nature and our desires.

It is good to remember that the mission of the Lamb was not just for us, his chosen people, but for all the world, all races, tongues, people and nations. The priestly reign of God's people is open to all the nations; no one can claim to have a monopoly on it. Later, as the seer gives us an image of the church, he will make that even more clear.

5:11-14

Angels now join the heavenly choir to form one more circle around the throne of God, and they compose a new hymn to Jesus which includes seven attributes, the symbol of perfect praise: power, riches, wisdom, strength, honor, glory and praise—all the endowments of a perfect leader, *the* perfect leader.

These angels will now enter powerfully into the drama of the earth's odyssey. Presently, as humanity is drawn higher and higher into the inner circle of the Lamb, the angels will begin to share an increasing part of their dignity with us until the final chapter of the book where they call us, interestingly, their fellow servants.

Praise, honor, glory and might; the number four always symbolizes the whole world. The praise inaugurated in heaven is then taken up by the earth to the resounding "Amen" of the four living creatures, the proclaimers of God's good news to the world. It is fitting that all of creation should break forth into a praise song; our eternal destiny is far greater than anything we can even imagine.

5

SECOND CYCLE—THE SEALS: REVELATION 6 AND 7

The frustration of the prophet, his inability to make sense out of life's sufferings, will now be examined in this cycle which looks at suffering in our human life. The first step in looking at the sickness that afflicts humankind is to look at the symptoms of that sickness, the seven areas of suffering, the full scope of suffering, in our life.

The seals have held closed the book of human history. It is suffering that makes life so unintelligible for us. If there were no suffering, there would not be so many anxious questions addressed to God or so much rebellion against him in the world. As we break open the seals—begin to understand them better—we discover in them the invitations of God in our life, to grow, to "come up higher" (Lk 14:10), to present ourselves to the sealing of the elect that will protect us for all eternity from the burden of suffering.

Suffering is the barbell of life that gives us spiritual muscle. "It was this that brought them before God's throne" (7:15). As we look at the times of great pain in our life, we are often surprised to discover that these were also the times of greatest growth. All of humanity is being purified in this crucible of suffering. All of humanity is invited to take part in the triumphant sealing that will bring that suffering to an eternal conclusion.

PART 4—SECOND CYCLE: THE SEALS

6:1-2

Already, in the first six seals, we have the whole drama of human history; the hatred, the wars, the hunger, the deaths, the persecutions, the fears. All that is negative is coming out like pus from a wound to be cleansed away once for all. It is as though the quota of human pain had to work itself up to a final eruption. No more can humanity hide its misery under a veneer of carefree joyfulness and comfortable living, the usual panaceas that hide inner pain but can only hide it for a short while.

In all of us there is the pain of the six seals, a pain that we try to cover over with greed or frivolity but that cannot go away until we are willing to face it and to do something about its root causes, human selfishness and human unwillingness to accept discipline in order to grow.

The living creatures, symbols of God's worldwide message and worldwide dominion, are the callers of the horsemen, an indication that the message they reveal is a message meant for all of humanity, not just for the Christian people. Indeed, suffering is a worldwide phenomenon and the Christians can hardly be said to have a monopoly on it.

The first seal, the horseman with a bow, may symbolize our human insecurity. Just as the arrows strike silently and suddenly, so tragedy is always a step away and may strike at any moment: accidents, fires, sickness. The arrows of the horseman are many and none of us can escape them for any great length of time. All our human pleasures are tinged with this dreadful insecurity which says to us on behalf of God: Not in this life is happiness to be found. Seek further!

6:3–4

The second seal, the rider with the sword, brings to mind the devastating power of human anger and its pent-up violence and potential for destructiveness. In all of us there is some element of that volcanic force. Who can escape it. The saints? All they could do was struggle against it by coming closer to God, the one healer. But from no one, not even from the saints, is the potential violence of anger completely driven away. It will work itself out either as constructive energy or as negative and hurtful behavior. And, since the first is the hardest, the second is very often what ends up being prevalent. This terrible second horseman has been scourging our world for countless centuries, and only the gentleness, the loving power of the Lamb can save us from its terrible consequences. "Love your enemy!" is the only answer to the rampaging anger in the human breast.

6:5-6

The third seal, the rider with the scales, calls to mind another great woe of humanity—the sense of loss, of deprivation, of having been cheated, of never having quite what one wants.

On the footsteps of human anger and rage comes human injustice. It is always the poor who are most victimized by the crimes, the wars, the violence in the world. It is not surprising that God's most tender concern is for the poor since they are called to suffer most from the uncertainties of the human condition.

No one, however, not even the wealthy, can escape the terrible hunger in the world, the sense that, no matter how much we have, we never have enough. Always, poverty is relative to the affluence I see around me. In some circles I may be poor if I only have one car or one house, whereas in other circles I may consider myself well off if I have a full meal every day. None of us ever seem to come to the moment when we can say, "I have enough. I want nothing more." Even the saint is dissatisfied and yearning for a more loving relationship, a greater personal holiness, a more perfect self-surrender. All of us have to weigh life on scales that are too small for our felt need.

6:7-8

The fourth seal, the rider named Death, carries his special horror for humanity. What greater fear is there in the human breast than the fear of death, of losing the tremendous gift of life, of sinking into non-existence? To a people created for eternal life, there is no greater, no more inexplicable tragedy than death. Only the Lamb's resurrection has taken some of the sting from death—but so little of the sting! It still remains perhaps the greatest fear of our humanity.

That fearful specter, Death, looms at every turn of the road of life. Swift as the arrow, cruel as the sword, slow and agonizing as the famine, it strikes everyone sooner or later and leaves no human life untouched. It is indeed possessor of authority over our thoughts, our actions, and our emotions.

6:9-11

The fifth seal, the complaint of the martyrs, speaks to us of the pain of having been treated unjustly. From our youngest childhood, the most poignant cry in our heart has been "It's not fair!" We have such a tremendous yearning to be treated fairly that nothing breaks our heart more than unfair treatment, unjust persecution, discrimination, the betrayal of a friendship we thought was secure, the disregard of our human rights. What wellsprings of misery there are in the call of the martyrs: "Master, avenge us!"

The advice to the martyrs is to be patient. When we see injustice triumph, when evil is profitable and holiness is punished, it is hard for us to be patient, to wait until God re-establishes the balance. It can be easy to slip into thinking we will not be avenged and justice will not triumph after all. Crushed under the altar of sacrifice, we often wonder if perhaps we are foolish for our trust in God, if triumph is not, after all, on the side of the powerful and the clever.

It seems, as perhaps God warns us here, that the number of the oppressed grows rather than diminishes. More and more, oppression makes inroads in the world and freedom disintegrates. The numbers of the persecuted are many and may become even more. But God whispers to all of them, to all of us: "Be patient! I know how to bring you to eternal consolation. There are crowns out there that still need to be conquered in my name." And all we can answer is, "I will wait." But oh how hard it is to wait!

6:12-17

The sixth seal, the terror of the people, is the awesome specter of fear that lies like a pall over all of humanity. Fear is our everyday companion—fear of accidents, of sickness, of poverty, of quarrels, of pain; fear with a well-known face and fear as a mysterious stranger. We who were created for eternal security seem

instead to have inherited unending insecurity and its accompany-
ing specter, fear. Furthermore, with all the fears that we endure,
we still have to be burdened with the fear of God, a fear that not
even the saints can escape completely. What if I have offended
him? What if I have failed to do his will? What if my sins remain
unforgiven? What if he has turned from me in anger and will no
longer listen to my call? What if, after all, the end will come without my having become fully converted?

Fear, ultimately, is the fear of a dead end, of coming to a point
where I can no longer cope, where I am eternally trapped in the
nightmare of frustration. To have failed forever with no further
hope of redemption is the ultimate fear of humanity.

There is a final seal yet to come which will usher in the seven
trumpets, and that is the burden of sin in the world, the fear that I
may lose my faith, that I may fall irretrievably into sin and lose
forever my relationship with God. These are the ills of humankind, the ills which only the Lamb who has gone through life,
death and resurrection can fully understand and therefore heal.

7:1-8

This chapter puts a new image on the concept of the seals. All
the human suffering exemplified in the six seals are ended by
the appearance of God's own seal which makes secure forever the
position of the saints. This is the seal that heals the slavery of the
other seals, the seals of human suffering. To all pain, God offers a
remedy; to all negatives, God presents an opposing positive that
renews our hope and our strength. It is interesting to note that this
sealing of God's people occurs before the seventh seal of the scroll
is broken, the seal which releases the punishment of God on sinful humanity.

The angels hold back the four winds, an image of sudden
silence. This is the silence of death which prepares the just for the
sealing of eternity. And it is also the silence of expectation; the
seventh seal is about to be broken, the seal of retribution against
sinners—the enslavers of humanity—and against sin—that
which in fact enslaves us all. But it is also the silence of shock at
the discovery of evil and sin and of its presence, not only out

there, but in our own heart. In receiving the seal of God, we also receive the revelation of our sins and their terrible consequences. Indeed, the seventh seal cannot be broken until God's grace makes it possible for us to understand the awesome burden of sin.

The one hundred and forty-four thousand are all the people of the world who believe in Jesus and who have been faithful to that belief. They will not be the only ones welcomed into heaven but they will be the first because they are the chosen ones. The imagery of this sealing is from Ezekiel 9:2–6 where those who have remained faithful to God are sealed with the awesome sign of the Tau. Imagery from the past comes forth to put deeper meaning into the events of the future. Those whose trust has been placed firmly in God will receive God's protection, even from the terrible ravages of sin in the world. Sin, even our own sinfulness, will not destroy us if we have chosen God as our bulwark and our foundation.

7:9–12

The group that now comes forward, so numerous that it cannot be counted, is made up of representatives from all the earth: nations (administrative boundaries), races (racial types), peoples (ethnic groups) and tongues (groups who share a common language). This group has a very special calling; it must acknowledge that "salvation is from our God who is seated on the throne, and from the Lamb." Why is this precisely the group that makes the profession of faith that might have been expected of the true Israelites (the faithful Christians) of the first group? I believe it is because these are the people who have lived a holy life on this earth without ever having known Jesus, hence, without ever having had the opportunity to proclaim him as Lord, something that all must do who would come to salvation. What could not be done on earth because of ignorance is now done in heaven where the non-Christian saints suddenly discover who it is that has brought them to salvation. In God's plan, there are none who cannot be saved if they have lived their ethics to the best of their ability.

Following the profession of faith of the multitude, the inner court of heaven now offers perfect praise to God (seven attributes) sandwiched in between two Amens that serve as an additional exclamation mark: let it be so! The attributes are separated into three groups; two, three, two. It might be stressing a point to search for a special reason for that triple division but, for us at least, it has a trinitarian flavor. The praise and the glory are set aside for God the Father, the creator. To the Son are attributed the wisdom (word of God), the thanksgiving (for redemption) and the honor (to one who has triumphed over death). The last two attributes are best suited to the Holy Spirit in whom is power and might with which to change the face of the earth and prepare humanity for the final coming of the Lord.

7:13-17

A dialogue now begins between the elder and the seer, between the church triumphant and the church militant. It is not an empty dialogue; it has a very special purpose. The challenge of the elder is for the seer (and with him for humanity) to examine who the members of the multitude might be. Why? Perhaps it is so we will know what good news it is that we have to bring to the world. The multitude obviously comes from all parts of the world (nations, races, people and tongues) and is composed of people who may be especially in need of hearing the good news since they are homeless, hungry, parched and afflicted by the burning sun. Who are these? To whom are we called to bring the message? Who needs to hear about the tremendous hope of salvation? Obviously those who don't know—the non-Christians. They have survived the great period of trial; they have lived life to the full with honor and integrity and, in doing so, "have washed their robes (a symbol of their personal dignity, their life's mission) in the blood of the Lamb," that blood which brings all to salvation, even those who do not know that it is what makes them clean and makes them deserving of heaven. It was this that brought them to the throne of God, not their faith in Jesus (whom they did not know) but their willingness to live life with integrity. Since Jesus was not able to shepherd them in this life, he will shepherd them in heaven along with his chosen Christian people.

6

THIRD CYCLE—THE TRUMPETS: REVELATION 8, 9, 10 AND 11

This cycle begins with a long pause of astonishment. We are now looking at the reality of sin in life, in our own life. At the sound of the trumpets, all the masks are falling and we are shown sin in all its ugliness. All of us are caught up in it. All of us harbor, in the abyss of our being, the terrible beast of sinfulness, that warped hunger to have our own way rather than to do things God's way. The sin of Adam is the sin of every human being. Nothing is harder for us to face than a God who will not be our servant but insists on remaining our master.

In the chapter of the two witnesses, we are given a look at two areas—the sins we commit and the sins that are committed against us. We are shown some of the sources of the self-hatred that we so often struggle against before we are given, in chapter 12, the key to overcoming that self-hatred.

This disquieting section ends with a heartening reminder. God is faithful; the ark of his covenant reminds us that he keeps forever before his eyes the promises he has made to us. We need not fear; God's guidance and protection will never be lacking in our life. Nothing, not even our sins, can keep us away from him.

PART 5—THIRD CYCLE: THE TRUMPETS

8:1-2

The seventh seal brings us into a new cycle—the awesome consequences of sin in our life. The silence in heaven is a silence of horror that sin should have brought us so much misery. It is also a silence of emphasis because what follows is of such tremendous importance. Trumpets, in scripture, are symbols of judgment. In this cycle, humanity is judged for the abysmal stupidity of living a life of sin.

8:3–5

The symbol of the gold censer is the power of the prayers of the saints to please God and to change the world. Before the disclosure of sin's tragedy, it is necessary for us to have an image of hope to hang on to. The censer is offered to God as a sweet fragrance. God hears the prayers of his holy people and finds them pleasing. Then the censer is poured out upon the earth, bringing cataclysmic results, that is, effecting powerful changes in humanity. It is important for us sometimes to reflect on the great power that there is in the sincere heartfelt prayers we offer to God for the welfare of others.

8:6–7

The first trumpet sounds and plagues reminiscent of the plagues of Egypt begin to afflict the earth. It is noteworthy that the first four trumpets speak of the affliction of nature, of the consequences of human sins, before those sins are brought to the forefront of the reflection. Before we can be enticed to look soberly at our sinfulness, perhaps it is important to realize what damages it can do in the world. Otherwise, there might not be enough incentive to bring us from sin to repentance and integrity.

Two symbols are presented to us. The first is hail, possibly a representation of pride and its ravages among the human community. People whose pride, arrogance and ambition beat down other people are a bane to community. They segment and separate people into classes, social status, ethnic preferences, all the things that militate against human cooperation and scorch the earth, that is, damage its fruitfulness. When people do not live in cooperation but are separated and filled with mutual distrust and rancor, the productivity of the earth is damaged, the harmony of nature is thrown off balance.

The second symbol we find in this passage is fire mixed with blood, an interesting image of human lust which also segments the human family. Infidelity, immorality, shallow self-serving relationships are the results of uncontrolled lust. Trust is destroyed, self-images are shattered, ethical values crumble, and the love of God is more or less abandoned. Like pride, lust shatters the community and wraps its adherents into self-centeredness. These two awesome evils destroy a third of the land or, in other words, diminish its ability to be productive for humankind by a third. The first has plunged us into countless wars and civil unrest and the second, of late, has fathered the terrible specter of AIDS. God has no need to punish us for our sins; we are quite capable of doing so ourselves.

8:8-9

The mountain of human pride and arrogance now hurls itself into the sea. We are reminded of the great naval powers that have confronted each other over the centuries and have filled the seas with carnage and blood, all in the name of domination and greed.

8:10-11

Science (the star) now enters into the fray and continues the ravaging of the earth by spilling its poisons (wormwood) into our streams and rivers, all in the name of progress and profit. Have not many of our industries been guilty of polluting the waters of the earth, causing fish to sicken and die and turning even drinking water into a dangerous liquid, filled with hazards to human health?

8:12

From land pollution and water pollution, we now turn to air pollution—acid rain, the destruction of the ozone, nuclear fallout. Human arrogance, greed and desire to control has succeeded in rendering even our air unsafe for humans. As the seer looks over the centuries, he has cause to shudder that human pride should have already brought so much damage to our earth—sea, land

and air. Nor is it likely that we have seen the end of it. Hence, nature will now turn to mourning the damage inflicted on it by humanity and pronounce a triple woe over human sin.

8:13

To use modern terminology, the eagle warns us that we haven't seen anything yet; the worse is still to come. Unless we stop using up our resources indiscriminately, polluting our planet and destroying its vegetation and animal life, we will find ourselves in a very uncomfortable position indeed. The cry of the eagle is the terror and the mourning of nature over what humanity is doing and how it is handling its sacred trust as steward of creation. Who will send us another Francis of Assisi to guide us back into the harmony with nature that, over the centuries, we have so sadly lost?

Sin carries a heavy burden. Having looked at some of the consequences of human folly that are already evident in our world, we will now turn to the inner ravages of sin in the human person so that, discerning it better, we may the sooner and the more eagerly come to conversion.

9:1-6

The first of the three woes is now upon us. A star, an angel of God, comes down to earth and flings open the door of the abyss, letting out billows of smoke so that the beast within can stand revealed. Having spoken of the damage of sin to ourselves and to the world, the seer now places us before the awesome abyss within our own heart where we have been nurturing evil, hiding it behind a veritable smokescreen comprised of all the rationalization we have used concerning our inner misery in order not to have to look at it too closely. When contact with God's angel happens, when we are called to conversion, then the smokescreen is removed and God forces us to look at the inner beast of our sins, sometimes causing us to wish we could die rather than face up to all that inner turmoil, inner hurt and inner self-centeredness that we have always suspected might be there but had never wanted to really look at previously.

The scorpion sting is remorse, the realization of how foolish we have been, of how much time we have wasted away from God, of how many people we have hurt. It is not a sting that kills but one that calls us to conversion. It will last only for a while and be replaced by the new life we will receive from God after we have brought the inner beast to the surface so we can look at it honestly and drive it out of our life. The five months is a significant symbol since five, in scripture, is a number that deals with ministry. The conversion experience, painful as it is, prepares us to begin fruitful ministry among the people of God.

The sealing of the saints has occurred, the prayers of the holy ones have been poured on the earth, and their merits have now revealed to us the source of our own suffering. We can no longer hide from it. As the smoke billows out, it hides everything (sun, air) except the realization of our inner misery. The moment of conversion is always a moment of intense self-awareness that tends to blot out everything else that is going on around us. The beast of my sins is no longer chained; it has been let loose to be examined, dealt with, and turned away from. No longer can I tolerate its presence in the murky cellar of my life.

9:7-11

Locusts are a good image for the accumulation of sin in our life because, individually, they are rather unimportant, but when they multiply they begin to devour everything in sight, to become the central focus of our life. In these particular sin-locusts, there is a great confusion, in fact complete confusion since there are seven symbols used. In these symbols, one can see the full scope of the inner ravages that sin brings into our life. The battle horses could be a symbol of hostility and belligerence, the chip-on-the-shoulder attitude toward life. The crowns are a symbol of pride and ambition, wanting to be better than others, wanting to control. The mixed men-women symbol speaks of the confusion of sexual roles—deviancy, sexism, the repression of one side or the other of our human personality that is exemplified by such terms as "macho" and "sex kitten." The lions' teeth symbolize cruelty and greed and the iron breastplate probably stands for defensiveness, insensitivity, isolationism in our life. The wings that roar like chariots are a good symbol of raging, bad temper, a bitter attitude toward life. And the stingers like those of scorpions convey to me the image of envy, gossipping, back-biting, pettiness. This is a rather sketchy list, and every other sin we could think of would probably fit in there somewhere. The locust is open to a wide interpretation of symbols.

Much more could be said about the beast of the abyss. Its seven parts convey the image of complete evil, complete confusion and also—once it is honestly looked at—complete remorse. Possibly the greatest torture we receive from the inner beast is the realization that we have fashioned it ourselves. As for the king of the locusts, the "Destroyer," he is the prince of sin who is constantly doing battle against us by whispering into our ears (like the locust wings) the allurement of sin and the promise of great ecstasy that is never fulfilled but always leaves instead the painful scorpion-sting of self-disgust and misery.

9:12–16

The sixth trumpet rouses the minions of war. Is there a greater plague on humanity than this nightmare of war? War comes in its proper time (hour, day, month, year), precisely when peace itself has become abominable because of the sins that it has given birth to. It is not a coincidence that the plague of war should come right after the enumeration of the sins that plague human beings. Sad to say, in our human history, peace is not always conducive to holiness—far from it! When there is peace, people become careless, unafraid of the consequences of their conduct and, it must be admitted, bored with life. When that happens, war becomes inevitable, as inevitable as the rampaging of two hundred million soldiers (the apparently irresistible thrust of war in the world) would be, to use the semitism applied here by the author.

Having prepared us for the vision of war, the author will now go on to describe its horror and also the fact that war, by itself, hardly ever makes people better but only increases the extent of rage that is in the world. The message for us is that, if we count on the pressure of war to bring people out of sin, we may find, in war, not the seed of justice but the seed of greater sin and the open invitation to more wars and more retaliations. No one ever wins a war; it only leaves losers of a lesser or greater degree.

The circle of evil that is described for us in chapters 8 and 9 is that sin brings misery to humanity and, if unchecked, leads inevitably to war. The hope that war will solve the problem is an illusion since war only brings greater misery. Greater misery leads to deeper sins and thus prepares the way to another war. There is no solution to sin except repentance. No one can ever be forced to live a holy life.

9:17–19

The breastplate of war is of three colors—the fiery red represents destruction and blood, the deep blue probably stands for death, and yellow is the symbol for famine. Destruction, death and hunger are the awesome consequences of the plague of war.

Not only does the impact of war kill and destroy but its aftermath is also deadly. The head is like a lion, roaring, charging, tearing, destroying, always hungry for more prey. The tail is like a snake, more subtle but no less deadly in its ability to kill and to poison life. Every war is followed by hunger and plague, not to mention the more subtle tragedy of human hatred sometimes so deep that a thousand years is not enough to wipe it out. No indeed, there are no winners in the nightmare of war.

9:20–21

The moral of this passage is that war never causes humanity to repent; it only makes people worse. In a negative vein so often used in scripture, the people are said not to have repented of six things, the number par excellence for imperfection. Two areas where repentance did not occur concern ideologies and the other four concern activities. Those who are guilty of these are bound to bring on themselves, over and over again, the nightmare of war.

The worship of demons is the first negative on the list. There is little that is more warped than to attribute to evil beings the power that belongs only to God. Those who worship demons do so for the power that they hope to obtain, and to receive that power they are often willing to go to great lengths in the pursuit of evil. Demonism is one of the most incomprehensible, most savage philosophies of life that our world can know.

False gods come next, and these are far more often worshiped than demons. They have many names: wealth, power, lust, success, control, materialism. There is a certain connection between the two ideologies listed here, and that connection, human greed, will become central in the ongoing message of the book.

The four negative activities that follow are murder, sorcery, fornication and theft, and these need little explaining except perhaps for sorcery which is not as easily discernible in our modern world and which perhaps centers around the areas of deception, lies, propaganda and what we now call brainwashing. Murder (especially the killing of defenseless civilians), sorcery (the lies, the betrayals, the psychological damage), fornication (as rape) and theft (the taking of booty, the annexation of land) all have a central role in the conduct of war. They are also at the core of much of the national hatred engendered by war (evidenced for instance in Psalm 137). As long as these remain unchecked, so will war, unfortunately, remain unchecked.

PART 6
INTERLUDES: THE SCROLL OF PROPHECY
AND THE WITNESSES

10:1-4

In this first interlude, there appear two witnesses to the will of God. The first is the angel of prophecy, and his message must be shared by the seer with peoples, languages, nations and kings, hence with all the world. The second is the seven thunders, the will of God as revealed in what Jesus called the "signs of the times." These are not to be shared (seal them up!), perhaps because the burden of discovering them rests on each individual person. Anyone is able to see what is going on around him or her, and therefore everyone is required to make a personal assessment of the situation. We are not under obligation to tell people things they can and should figure out for themselves.

Much imagery surrounds the angel of prophecy, the heavenly revealer of the divine will. His face is like the sun; he gazes upon the things of God and he has first-hand knowledge of heavenly realities. And his feet are columns of fire; he will bring a cleansing, purifying element to the earth. As God's prophetic word stands revealed, it burns away all that is sinful and negative. In another vein, one might say that the prophetic panorama of salvation history spans heaven (the sun) and hell (the fire). Nothing is outside of God's ability to govern and to accomplish his will.

The Shekinah envelops the prophetic messenger; the word is indeed the word of God, hiding/revealing the presence of God within it. And the word is the revelation of God's faithfulness to his covenant (the rainbow), a reminder to us that, whatever happens, God will not forget or fail to accomplish what he has promised us. There is power in the prophecy (the roar of the lion), a power that spans the sea (chaos and also the totalitarian Roman empire) and earth (the ever-present menace of invasion from the east, hence the symbol of war). God's will is going to be accomplished in spite of (perhaps even with the tool of) chaos and war. Everything inevitably furthers the plan that was formulated in heaven before the creation of the world.

10:5–7

The messenger of the Lord now takes an oath to accomplish the plan of God without delay. There is a sense of renewed urgency. God's will must be done; humanity's happiness depends on it.

We are always challenged to discern the difference in our life between a necessary interlude and an unnecessary delay. An interlude is the time it takes me to acquire the skills I will need in the service of the Lord. Delay is a matter of going after unimportant distractions and sinful (or at least unfruitful) pleasures. Delay is what happens when I am reluctant to enter into the plan of God, when I hesitate to accept the scroll of prophecy (a vocation?) that has been handed to me, to serve the people of God and to work for justice in the world.

The more overwhelming I sense the task to be, the more likely I am to indulge in delays. Also, the more I assume I must do it all by myself, the more reluctant I am likely to be in starting out. Much depends on my ability to see myself simply as a tool of God in the accomplishment of his will and to realize that he is quite able to handle any problems that come along as the task progresses and to give me the time, wisdom and energy I need to accomplish his work.

I think what robs me of time and energy the most is wanting to have my own way and fearing that, if I don't, I have failed in my mission. To serve God without delay requires that I be attuned to his will and comfortable with doing things his way. It is not wise for me to assume too quickly that I know what is success and what is failure when it comes to the service of God. If I remain close to the Lord and if his glory is all I seek, everything will be success, even what I consider failure.

10:8-11

As he accepts the scroll, the seer experiences the paradox of ministry. It is sweet to the taste to be a servant of God but oh how sour to the stomach to so often have to announce bad news to our people! It is the burden of the minister to want the best for others and to realize that their conduct so often predisposes them for the worst. If the minister speaks up, as indeed he must, he is seen as a spoilsport, a criticizer, a pessimist. The sweetness of our mission is that we are called to announce the great love of God for all his creation; the sourness is that we must remind people of the grave danger of sin and the need for repentance. We serve a God who cannot and will not tolerate injustice.

A feature of this book is the presence of a certain "someone" who often acts as a catalyst toward the prophet. "Someone" speaks to him, "someone" hands him a measuring rod, etc. Sometimes it is a voice that speaks or an elder or an angel, none of whom are specifically identified. This is of course a device to keep the flow of the message going but I think there is a symbolism in it also. In life, there are many forces, many suggestions, many events that lead us in one direction or another without our really knowing how it has all come about. All the events that surround my life speak God's will to me, and the better I am at listening, the more my life will be fruitful and successful.

The prophecy entrusted to the seer is for all peoples, nations, languages and kings (government leaders). Again, the number four appears in relation to universality. The message is for everyone and it cannot exclude anyone. God does not call us to ministry for the sake of the few but for the sake of all humanity. The servant of God must be beyond provincialism; he belongs to the world.

11:1–2

In preparation for the ideological struggle that is described in this second vision, the seer gives us an image of the temple of Jerusalem as the symbol of the human person. The holy of holies is that deeper part of ourself where the Christ is enthroned forever and will never be dislodged. The more we stand worshiping before our Lord, the less we are likely to be affected by the outward turmoil of our life and of our world. The court of the priests surrounds the holy of holies, and this refers to our religious practices which nourish and strengthen our union with the Lord. The third court, the court of the Israelites, refers to our ethical values, our ideals. These three areas stand under the protection of God, and the more we live within them, the more our life will be secure.

And now we come to the fourth court, the court of the Gentiles. This refers to our worldly pursuits, our interactions of the marketplace, so to speak—the civil laws, the government structures, the capitalism, the dog-eat-dog aspects of life where we are always under some form of persecution, all the more so if we hold to our ethical values and our faith convictions very strongly. A deeply religious person is often suspicious to power-people and generally a detriment to the merchant element with its enticements to us to surround ourselves with material goods and to find in these our happiness and our self-esteem. Little wonder, then, that these two elements, power and greed, are going to rise up now and strive to overcome the witnesses of God's values in the world.

Lest we become smug, we need to remember that the ideological clash in the court of the Gentiles is also an inner conflict because that is the level where we struggle with personal pride, ambition, sinful habits, imperfections that often are a greater cause of persecution to us than anything we experience on the outside. Always we find ourselves torn between the ideals we strive to live by and the weaknesses within us that cause us to fall short of what we hope to do and to be. There is a tendency in us to spend a great deal of time and energy trying to overcome these negatives, and we often become frustrated because they seem always to be there. It is good to remember that these things are really superficial. Our call is to live our life in the presence of the Lord and to allow him to remove the negatives from us at his own leisure. If our choice is staunchly for God, there are no negatives, no faults in our life that can ever keep us from him. What is most important is not that we be perfect but that, in spite of all, we remain faithful.

11:3-11

This long and rather obscure prophecy is open to various interpretations and it is hard to say which of these is most prominent in the mind of the writer. Perhaps no interpretation we give will do full justice to the text or solve all its questions. Who are the two witnesses? If, as tradition has stated, they are Enoch and Elijah, then they represent the traditions on which our life is built and the prophecy element, our hopes and dreams for the future and our hunger for perfect justice in the world. In opposition to them stands the wicked city with its two names, Sodom and Egypt, clearly the symbols of sin and persecution. Sin represents all the ways in which we mess up our life, and persecution, of course, is the way others try to mess up our life for us.

Interestingly, when I fall into either of those two traps, I get caught up in the present, and tradition and prophecy in my life both come under attack. Taking sin as the first example, when I fall into sin, I am wrapped up in the present moment with often little concern for the traditions in my life—rules, laws, beliefs. Sin always makes me reluctant to consider the ethical values on which I have strived to build up my life or the ideals I have set before me. Hence, as sin makes me reluctant to consider my traditions, so it makes me unwilling to look at the prophecy side of my life, what I would like to become, the justice I ought to establish, my hopes for eternal life. The more I give in to sin, the more I try to destroy (or at least to forget) the traditions and the ideals of my life and my inborn desire to live in justice.

Looking at the "Egypt" symbol, when we try to enslave other people, we also strike out at those two areas of their life: we try to convince them that their beliefs are worthless (tradition) and we try to destroy any hopes they have of bettering their life (prophecy). The methods of dictatorships, whether right-wing or left-wing, are the same: enslave the people by destroying their self-worth and any hope they may have for the future. Extremist governments are usually anti-religion (unless they can control the religion) and against the betterment of the poor (the less dependent the people, the harder to control).

Perhaps the best news in the passage is that, ultimately, those tactics don't work. You cannot destroy people's traditions and you cannot kill their hopes completely. These always resurrect to challenge the oppressors. No one can, or will, bury them, that is, eliminate them in the human person, no matter how much they might wish they could.

The exchange of gifts, the eat-drink-and-be-merry philosophy, stands in stark contrast to the sackcloth of the witnesses. A life built on sound traditions and firm hopes is always a disciplined life. When one is wrapped up in sin or suffering under oppression, short-term pleasures are what is sought. We try to make up in abundance of goods and experiences for the permanence that is lacking. The less we are faithful to the past, the less hope we have in the future, the more we concentrate on the materialism of the present. Bread-and-circuses philosophies are always central to sin and oppression.

11:12–14

The two prophets recreate the ascension of Jesus; they go up to heaven as others look on. But, here, it is not the friends who look on but the enemies. When Jesus ascended to heaven, the witnessing of the experience was only for his friends because he did not wish to force his enemies to believe. But here it is the enemies who look on because they need to be made aware of the importance of tradition and prophecy in the human experience, that it is indeed what lifts us to heaven, helps us to transcend the human condition.

Symbols abound in this short passage. A tenth of the city falls into ruin. Since the city is a symbol of worldliness, we are reminded that some of that worldliness must be sacrificed if we are to come to any relationship with God. Ultimately, everything must die that stands in God's way (seven thousand—the number seven again, the complete number). The longer it takes us to come to God, the more failure and disappointment we may have to experience. Until everything has been removed that keeps us from God, we have not yet fully come to conversion.

That thought brings us to the final reflection. The people worship God out of fear. Certainly, if we will not worship God out of love, we will be forced to worship him out of fear, as usually happens at times of crises and catastrophe. The problem with that kind of worship is that, by itself, it is too shallow. If it does not lead us to worship God out of love, we will only abandon God again after the crisis is passed. If catastrophe does not cause us to enter into a love-relationship with God, we may be headed for other, and greater, catastrophes. If we have not benefited from the second woe, beware! The third woe is quickly coming. And the third woe is a deepening of our spiritual misery. Nothing in this life brings us to fullness of peace and of happiness except a sincere and abiding love for God.

11:15-18

Once again a cycle ends with the end of the world, with the inevitable triumph of the creator-God who, in spite of our pride, our rebellion and our anger, has still brought the world to the point where he had willed to bring it. No matter how much we struggle against God, we all must come to the moment of surrender, to death which plunges us unprotected into the presence of God. The kingdom of the earth must of necessity belong to God because all of its citizens, none excepted, will eventually stand helpless before God. That is our destiny. We can choose either to embrace it or to fight against it but we can never escape it.

In the hymn of triumph of the elders, there is a disquieting statement: "The nations have raged in anger." What is this anger of the world against God? Where does it come from and what has given it birth? It is an anger that began, according to Genesis, at the very dawn of humanity when the first couple sought to be freed of the jurisdiction of God by grasping a power equal to his. The original sin of humanity is the sin of the first Adam, the desire to control God, to trick him into becoming our servant rather than our master.

Why such a presumption in the human psyche? Perhaps its root reason is to be found in the foundational quality of our creation, that we are created in the image and the likeness of God. There is in every human heart an awesome hunger for divinity. We want to be the very best, the wisest, the most powerful, the wealthiest, the most perfect human being in the world. In short, we want to be God because we have been created to be like God. The divine image is the only one that really fits in our life.

We rage against God because we feel that, somehow, we have been betrayed. We are no better than anyone else, and no more loved. We have been created for perfection and we are doomed to live in a world that always remains imperfect. We want to be in control, even of God, and we cannot even control our own life. Humanity, therefore, often finds itself saying "There is no God!" because that is still easier than to say, "There is a God and I can't control him."

With all our hunger for divine perfection, we find ourselves in relationship with a God who tells us that we are no better than anyone else in the world, that we are no more precious to him than even the most insignificant human being, that wealth is meaningless and we really only own that which we are willing to let go of, that hatred is evil and unforgiveness is forbidden, that revenge belongs to him and not to us, that inevitably we will come to the moment of death. The nations rage against a God who has created them for perfection and left them imperfect, who has created them for eternal life and left them mortal. We live in a paradox, and because we cannot see beyond the paradox to the infinitely wise reason for what seems unreasonable, we are constantly experiencing alienation from God—and anger.

There is only one answer, really, a simple answer but one that we find singularly difficult. We must wait trustingly for God to give us that for which we have been created. We must accept the power of powerlessness. We must realize that happiness does not lie in perfection but rather in relationship, that it is not control that fulfills us but the ability to let go.

The sin of Adam may be said to be twofold. It is first of all the pride of wanting to be God, to be in control, to be the best. It is also the terrible fear that our hopes may be in vain, that after all we may be headed for an eternal disappointment. We find it hard to believe that a God we cannot control is a God we can still count on implicitly. In the human rage, there is this very great difficulty we experience when we are faced with the fact that we are irremediably vulnerable and that, want it or not, we must put our trust in God.

Perhaps the third woe is exemplified here in the phrase, "the time to destroy those who lay the earth waste." What a tragedy to come to the end of life and realize that we have failed, that for all eternity we must live in the realization that we could have made it, that all the opportunities were there for us, and that we still chose against God and therefore against life. Hell is the eternal obligation to live in self-hatred and self-blame, with the clear realization of what could have been if only we had been willing to allow it.

11:19

The ark of the covenant is the proof that God is faithful, a proof we will receive, for our rejoicing or our consternation, when death ushers us into eternal life. All the promises will be fulfilled for those who have believed the promises. For the others, there will only be the "gnashing of teeth," the eternal rage over the failure they have themselves chosen.

Lightning, thunder, earthquake, hail now break forth—a representation of all the forces of nature celebrating the eternal triumph of God. All the time when we thought we had subdued the world, the world was still obeying only God.

If, then, we arm ourselves with patience and faith, we can wait to receive from God freely that which we so often frustrate ourselves trying to attain on our own. The anchor of our faith is that God is eternally faithful. If we live in that faith, we will receive the reward of "the prophets and the holy ones," of those whose vision of the future is not clouded by pride and self-centeredness but is directed completely toward God who is our beginning, our sustenance and our end.

7

FOURTH CYCLE—THE SIGNS: REVELATION 12, 13, 14 AND 15

We now enter the center of the chiastic structure and also the center of the message of the book. In this cycle, we will be given a look at the ideological struggle that is going on in the world between the dragon and the Lamb, between worldly greed and spiritual idealism. In a series of powerful images, the writer will outline for us the scope of that struggle and the rage against humanity of the "ancient enemy" who sees his sway over the world threatened by the redemptive work of the Lamb of God, the Lord Jesus Christ.

John will unmask for us some of the wiles of our spiritual enemy and some of the weaknesses within us that he exploits in his effort to lead us away from what would bring us life and true happiness. He is the negative force in the world, the rebellious anger against God that has infiltrated the human race from its very beginning. He is the shadow side of the human reality.

Two interconnected images will be introduced as the special witnesses of the dragon; worldly oppressive power (the beast from the sea, that is from chaos) and the greed for wealth (the beast from the earth, that is from Sheol, the land of illusion). The need to control and the desire for pleasure are the hooks by which the enemy ensnares humanity and at whose service much of our time and a large measure of our resources are spent.

The final part of the cycle is the responding voices from heaven, calling us to judgment, issuing to us a solemn invitation to put our trust in God the judge who alone knows the center of our heart and what it really takes to bring us to happiness.

The most positive and exhilarating sign of this cycle is the harvest of the earth which is, in my opinion, one of our primary reasons for placing our trust in the judgment of God rather than casting our lot with the worldly allurements of control (chaos) and wealth (illusion). In the fourth cycle, the writer of Revelation undoubtedly reaches the heights of his holy eloquence.

PART 7—FOURTH CYCLE: THE FIRST THREE SIGNS

12:1-6

The cycle of the seven signs is of special importance in the book of Revelation because it is the center of the chiasmus and therefore the center of the message that the book wants to convey. Here we have the core of the ideological warfare that is being carried on between God who seeks to liberate humanity and Satan who seeks to enslave it. Everything that has come before has been leading up to this cosmic clash. Everything that comes after speaks of the ways it is resolved inevitably in God's favor and therefore in favor of the liberation of humanity.

The cycle begins with two signs in paradoxical positions which are really part of the first sign—the woman who is on the side of good and the dragon who is on the side of evil, the woman who exalts humanity and the dragon who sweeps it downward to the earth. The woman is a composite figure and probably stands for three different images. She is the Old Testament giving birth to the New Testament, she is Mary giving birth to Jesus, and she is also the church giving birth to Christianity in the world. The symbols in Johannine literature are always to be read on several levels of reality. This versatile cosmic woman is clothed with the sun— that is, the presence of God is all around her, she is safely under divine protection. The moon is beneath her feet. The moon is the symbol of night, of darkness, of sorcery, of all those forces in opposition to God, and these the woman has firmly under her feet; she has control over them and she scorns them.

The twelve stars around the woman's head are a well-known symbol in Marian art. As the number twelve attests, these are the Christian people whom she exalts and who are her crown. She is pregnant with the divine life and is constantly seeking to give birth to Jesus in the world, to make him more powerfully present.

Opposing the woman is the second sign which is her counterpart—her shadow, to use modern terminology. The dragon is Lucifer, the fallen angel who seeks to drag down the stars (the people of God) from heaven to earth, from holiness to sin and to selfishness. The dragon is red, the color of violence, of rage, of rebellion. He has seven heads, a symbol of absolute intellectual pride and arrogance, and ten horns, the ten emperors who serve him and who will be mentioned over and over again in this cosmic struggle, the ten emperors who, for us, represent the ten general persecutions of the church under Roman rule. The seven crowns again remind us of the dragon's pride and also of his authority over worldly people, of his fatal hold on the world, of his lust to control life. This dragon wants to destroy the Christ-life in the world that liberates people and removes them from the grasp of the satanic forces.

The contrast between the two paradoxical signs continues. The dragon who was born in heaven is hurled down to earth and the child who was born on earth is caught up to heaven. The dragon seeks to control the world, but the world has been given over to the holy child who is called to shepherd all nations. Try as he might, the dragon cannot win over the child just as tyranny cannot win over human hope. The will of God is inevitable.

The woman flees into the desert; the church enters its period of purification and growth in holiness. The church cannot leave the desert until it has truly become holy; otherwise it is at the mercy of the dragon who strives to destroy it by instilling in its very members the spirit of greed and self-centeredness. Always the church has to undergo purification because the church is always persecuted, from outside and, far more dangerously, from within. The twelve hundred and sixty days (the three and a half years of persecution) represent all the history of the church until its final triumph. There has always been persecution and there will always be persecution, but God takes care of his church and continues to purify it, making use of the very persecutions meant to destroy the church in order to deepen its holiness. The paradox of history is that the church is holiest when it is most persecuted.

The dragon will always wound but he will never kill. So God has willed it, and he is the one who is in charge.

12:7-9

The contrast between good and evil is not just on earth; it is also in heaven. The angel of death is confronted by the angel of life, the seducer of humanity is overpowered by the protector of humanity. Ultimately, the balance between good and evil will always be tipped on the side of good. There is no place for the devil in heaven; there he cannot prevail. That is the good news for us. When we enter heaven, we will forever be free of the attacks of the seducer. The bad news, of course, is that, since he cannot prevail in heaven, the dragon will carry out his struggle against God on earth where the forces he encounters are far less overwhelming, and there he will try to destroy the harmony of creation by destroying the harmony placed by God within the human heart.

The drama begins in a garden, the garden of Eden, where the ancient serpent seduces the woman and, with her, humanity. The drama has its turning point in another garden, Golgotha (see Jn 19:41), where a woman defeats the serpent by accepting the words of the Lord, "Behold your son!" (Jn 19:26) and thus bringing all of humanity into kinship with God and thereby giving to all of us an inalienable right to be in heaven, in that heaven from which Satan has been driven because of his pride and his rebellion. Thus, the drama will end in a garden, in the eternal Eden of heaven.

12:10-12

All of us are familiar with the accuser, that inner voice that keeps telling us we are not good enough, we are not trying hard enough, we don't love enough. All the "shoulds" we throw at ourselves are the voice of the accuser trying to discourage us from serving God by telling us we are not worth loving and we are simply not deserving of heaven.

The only way to defeat this inner accuser is through "the blood of the Lamb." The way of Satan, pride, is that desire to appear better than we know ourselves to be, to put on a mask, to try to fool others about who we really are. Pride urges us to prove ourselves better than others because, deep inside, we feel we may not be as good as others. And so we put up a front, we try to impress people by our words or our actions, we spend much time and energy trying to prove ourselves right and others wrong. The net result of all that is to alienate ourselves from others, to destroy our link with the community, to hamper the work of God in the world. Sadly, the voice that tells us we are not good enough for God also leads us into behavior that alienates us from God. It contains its own self-fulfilling prophecy.

The way of the Lamb is the way of humility, that profound realization that, since God made us, we are good enough and we must be faithful to what we have been created to become. It is as ourselves that we are most admirable, not when we try to be someone else. Humility brings us into good relations with our community. If we are not afraid to be known, then we can afford to communicate. If we really do believe we are good enough for God, then we must also believe that others are good enough for God and therefore worthy of our love and our respect. We defeat the accuser by the blood of the Lamb, by this profound realization that we are good enough for God, that in fact we are worth dying for. God could give us no greater proof of his love than that. In this tremendous revelation from God, our real worth is uncovered and the lies of the devil are unmasked. He can never have power over us again, and so all he can do is stir up opposition to us, try to win us over by fear if not by persuasion.

The fury of the devil is understandable when we realize that he has been unmasked and that he has only a short lifetime to win us away from God. When death comes, God's love will triumph and no lies can ever turn us away from him again. In heaven we will be eternally safe. Hence the devil's eagerness to accuse us, to try to discourage us from continuing in the service of God. Our great enemy is discouragement and that self-hatred which is always a subtle criticism of God. After all, if I am not good enough for heaven, what does that say about the One who has created me for the purpose of bringing me into the enjoyment of heaven?

If our trust is truly in God, then, like the woman, we are clothed with the sun and we have nothing to fear from the darkness. Hope is the center of our heart and joy is our treasure. The only thing that conquers the accuser is the laying down of our life at the feet of God, the echoing with all our heart of the tremendous words of Jesus: "Father, into your hands I commend my spirit" (Lk 23:46).

12:13-17

Perhaps what this passage really illustrates for us is our reason for calling Satan a "poor devil." The demonic dragon is burning with impotent rage. Everything he attempts leads to deeper frustration, deeper self-hatred, and more glorious triumph for God's holy people. The cards are stacked against evil, not in its favor.

Possibly the greatest frustration of those who choose evil is that, basically, evil does not work. It leads to self-hatred which leads to greater evil which leads to deeper self-hatred. If the chain of evil is not broken, it will lead those who have embraced it to eternal frustration which is hell. Because evil leads to frustration, it also leads to rage against the people who live a holy life because a holy life does work and does make people happy. It can be a great frustration for people boiling with self-hatred to see how happy others really are. Hence the temptation to "take them down a peg" and destroy the harmony of holiness.

The woman, symbol of all that is holy in humanity, is seen as the enemy by the dragon. She represents everything that the dragon is not and, by that fact, adds to his self-hatred. She exalts humanity whereas he strives to humiliate it; she gives life while he seeks to give death; she loves and he hates. In all things she stands as his opposite. She is protected by God; nature is on her side; everything seems to work for her, even the persecutions fomented by the dragon. Filled with a self-loathing that grows from seeing in the woman all that he ought to be but does not wish to become, the dragon strikes at her, trying to destroy her. Holy people always stand as a condemnation of evil ways, and those who have chosen evil ways can be very threatened by holiness. The atheists have a burning desire to destroy religion; they are not content just to ignore it. As long as it stands, and triumphs, goodness appears as an accusation of their ways and their chosen beliefs, or rather their choice not to believe.

To strike at the woman, the dragon calls forth a torrent of water, symbol of the power of chaos in the world. The dragon sends suffering to God's holy people in an effort to turn them from God. He sends us pain, temptation, a sense of outrage, all the sufferings so well depicted in the second cycle. But holiness has the earth on its side. Nature favors those who live in harmony with it; their health is better, their life is more successful in the ways that matter, they form more powerful friendships, their peace is more profound. Ultimately, time stands on the side of holiness. To quote a saying-reversal; "Time wounds all heels." Evil carries its own punishment just as surely as holiness carries its own reward. No matter how much the dragons of this world try to hurt others, they will always end up hurting themselves the most.

The dragon now takes up his position on the seashore, symbol of instability, of the shaky position of evil in the world. Evil always lives on the edge of chaos, of self-destruction. The weapons that hate-filled people use against others—lies, persecution, oppression—always end up engulfing those who make use of them. Perhaps one of the reasons why evil is always self-destructive is that we tend to hate in others the very things we hate in ourselves, and thus, in persecuting others, we are also persecuting ourselves. Hatred, which has at its core rebellion against God's will for his creatures, cannot be anything but self-destructive.

13:1–4

The second and third signs of this cycle make up chapter 13 and they are integrally entangled with one another. Together they represent the underpinning of evil that comes forward to fight against the plan of God for the world. The first four verses are a description of the beast from the sea. Geographically, for Asia Minor, the sea is synonymous with the west, and therefore here it represents the Roman power. Taken in its greater context, this beast represents all civil powers, especially those that hold oppressive sway over their people. The description is telling: a beast like a leopard, with all the swiftness, the cunning, the restlessness and the cruelty ascribed to that beast, paws like a bear, insensitivity in its dealings with people and great power to oppress, mouth like a lion, that is, a great amount of greed for wealth, for power, for luxury. In a greater or lesser measure, this composite beast pretty well describes all governmental authority in the world, past and present.

The diadems and the heads have a lot to do with the historical context in which the book was written, but there is also a prophetic flavor to it if we reflect on the fact that there were ten major persecutions of the church in Roman times, hence ten emperors who made a concentrated effort to destroy the church. But this attack against God by worldly powers did not stop with the collapse of the Roman empire; it is still very much in evidence in the world. The blasphemous names are still being proclaimed, be they communism, socialism, capitalism, imperialism, or whatever political shape each nation chooses to take. Sooner or later the will of God as expressed through his church will run counter to the ambition of worldly leaders and a persecution, overt or subtle, will follow.

There is something noteworthy about the statement that men worshiped the beast (not "people" but "men"). I believe it is men, not women, who most thoroughly buy into the power of the state and uphold its supremacy within the countries of the world. Women are far less inclined to follow power blindly than men are, perhaps because, as homemakers, they are more concerned with the health of the society than with its power. It is men who are the empire builders of the world, not women. The veneration of power and the blind following of charismatic leaders is one of the traps men are the most susceptible to get into.

13:5–8

The proud boast of the beast (government) is that it is right and that it has all the answers. One only needs to listen to a political speech to hear that boast being proclaimed, and indeed one cannot imagine that politicians really have any alternatives if they want to be elected and followed in their policies. The second kind of governmental proclamation is more sinister since it deals with blasphemies, that is, with the argument that the hopes of humankind reside in following it rather than following God. When a government begins to make itself god to the people, then we have a door wide open to tyranny. Nor is it necessary that the government actually deny God. Very often its claim is rather that God is on its side, in its service, so to speak, as is the case in fanatical countries. The only good news here is that tyranny is self-eliminating; eventually it does not work and it must phase itself out. It is too great a strain on a government to maintain tyranny; it must either loosen the controls or face a revolution. Hence, we have here the assurance that the tyranny will not last beyond forty-two months (symbolic of a time of persecution, courtesy of Antiochus Epiphanes of unlamented memory).

Every country in the world will, at one time or another, know some form of tyranny. There is no "race, people, language or nation" that is immune to this pervasive desire to claim a divine right to control. People who do not have a loving relationship with God (whose names are not in the book of the living) are always susceptible to being swayed by the boasts and blasphemies of governments groping for the consolidation of power. If it is not God who is our God, then we must of necessity search for a substitute god somewhere else, none of us being really sufficient unto ourselves.

13:9–10

This short commentary is a reflection by the author on the situation he has just outlined. There will be another such reflection after the mention of the second beast. The seer muses on the inevitability of persecution if one is faithful to one's ethical and spiritual values. There are two forms of persecution that the state can use in order to impose its claim to supremacy. The state can react with pressure on the dissenters, here listed as captivity. To disagree with the state's policies can land one in jail or at least under whatever legal pressures the state can impose, sometimes even under such a subtle pressure as blacklisting. We have only to think of what can happen to social protesters and sanctuary providers in this country to realize that no one is immune to the pressure to conform to the will of the state.

The other form of persecution is more direct; it involves physical violence, the ideal tool of fanatical governments that often consider individual lives as unimportant in comparison with the will of the state. If people will not conform, they will be eliminated. The holocaust of Nazi Germany and the systematic genocide of Stalin's Russia are sad examples of that abuse of power by tyrannical states. Making God first in our life can have some serious consequences for us.

13:11-14

Coming forth in support of the first beast (power) is the second beast, sprung from the earth. This beast is commerce, wealth, the merchant element of humanity, seat of so much greed, and which cannot flourish except under a strong government. Hence commerce places itself at the service of power so that it may continue to accumulate wealth. How often the wars started by the power people of government are really instigated by the wealth element of commerce looking for the protection of its own investments or the growth of its opportunities! This second beast is described in simple but interesting terms. It has the horns of a ram, the ability to bulldoze anything or anyone that stands in its way, and the speech of a dragon, the ability to convince people it has invincible power to take care of all the needs of humanity. Commerce uses the authority of government for its own purpose, giving support and wealth to the government in exchange. These two elements of society are always closely tied to one another and, when one suffers, the other suffers also, as will be exemplified for us in the dirge of chapter 18.

This second beast can perform great prodigies. Science is at its service and, through science, truly miraculous achievements happen. The first of these listed here is fire from heaven, which we can readily identify as the marvel of electricity. Other marvels will be achieved by science and at least one of these will be specifically listed as in the service of power although, implicitly, all scientific progress is at the service of both power and wealth. We have seen in the last century or so how much stock has been placed in science's ability to be a God-replacement for humanity, hence an idol. People have placed their hope in science and conveniently ignored God. Slowly, however, it is beginning to dawn on us that science can kill as well as heal, that it can cause even greater problems than those it has cured. Our idol of science has indeed been found to have feet of clay.

13:15-18

The beast from the earth is the beast from Sheol which is the land of illusion and of ultimate despair. Hence, the second beast fashions an image of the first beast (the illusion of life) to which it gives the power of speech and the power to control the lives of people and to place life and death on the level of obedience to its whims. This image is the ideological warfare that is being waged in the world between God and his enemy, an ideological warfare into which each and every one of us is entangled by the very fact that we are humans, created in the image of God (the opposite to the image of the beast) and therefore representing a threat to the enemy of God. The image that is given the power of speech has a disturbing resemblance to the marvel of television with its power to manipulate life, to shape the ethics of people and, above all, to serve the interests of commerce as is easily seen by the countless commercials and their blatant appeal to human greed. It does not take much television viewing for us to get the message that the only people who are anybody are those who have the power and the wealth and that the others, the losers in the struggle for domination, are as good as dead. Then, when the poor and the powerless grasp for those things by the only means available to them— crime—we condemn them for stealing the very things we have convinced them they cannot do without.

This human greed, it will be easily guessed, is the real mark of the beast, that mysterious six six six that represents imperfection (one short of the perfect number which is seven) on the ideological level (three, the symbol for theological truth). Six six six, then, is the ultimate lie, and that lie is that wealth and power are the givers of happiness rather than God. That is the focus of the cosmic struggle between good and evil and it has been going on for at least as long as recorded history.

In the book of Revelation, every spiritual truth has its shadow side, its counterpart in the realm of darkness. There is a Holy Trinity, Father, Son and Spirit, and a trinity of evil, Satan, the beast, and (as yet to be encountered) the false prophet (antichrist). We have the angel of light and the angel of darkness. We have the holy Mother and the whore. We have the sealing of the elect and, here, the sealing of the followers of evil. The book always offers a balance between good and bad, between the reality and the illusion. It is no wonder that we are so often led astray when we consider that evil always in some way mirrors the good it is trying to supplant. In the temptation in the desert, we learn that it is not only Jesus who can quote scripture; the devil can match him quotation for quotation. What makes evil so ominous is the difficulty we so often have in distinguishing it from good. All life has its shadow, what we might call the imitation of life, and we are often tempted to follow the shadow which always appears far more obtainable than the life it mirrors. Looking for a short-cut to perfection can leave us wide open to the machinations of the devil.

The image of the beast, in the context of the book, is emperor-worship, that form of social idolatry that has led to the seer's persecution because of his unwillingness to go along with it. It is the image of power and wealth as god. The demonic six six six of human greed is placed on one of two parts of the human body, the head or the hand. The mark on the head relates to our intellect, our cleverness, our knowledge, our leadership ability at the service of power. It can be equated with what we call the scientific revolution which has so often provided the weapons for power and for wealth. The mark on the hand represents our work, our crafts, our physical labor which is so often at the service of power (as in war situations) and of wealth (the automation of labor). Its equation, obviously, is the industrial revolution that has brought in so many luxuries and, with them, the illusion that we can do nicely without God.

In the center of the chiasmus, then, we are presented with a clear choice between the two beasts of power and wealth and the following of the Lamb, membership in the one hundred and forty-four thousand of the church. The choice is not as easy to make as we might think because the warfare is not just carried out in the world but also in our own heart. We may profess the Lord with our lips but, even as we do so, we often grasp for power and for our share of worldly luxuries. Witness the lifestyle of even some of our most dedicated Christian leaders. None of us is as free from the struggle as, unwisely, we sometimes allow ourselves to think.

PART 8—FOURTH CYCLE: THE LAST FOUR SIGNS

14:1-5

We are now introduced to the fourth sign, and we are faced with a hymn which we are not worthy to hear because we have not yet completed our surrender to the Lord. This hymn, the hymn of the elect, can be heard only in heaven where we will be pure and perfect for all eternity. This hymn will be accompanied by the sound of thunder (God's infinite power) and music (humankind's adoration)—a perfect blend.

This is a triumphal image of redeemed humanity enjoying the eternal protection of the Lamb and settled firmly on the heights of Zion, the place where God and humanity meet in an eternal interaction. We are given a stark, simple image of heaven offered in a few symbolic words that conceal more than they reveal since the hymn which is the heart of this eternal triumph cannot be heard by us yet. Without the hymn, all the joy and the happiness remain unsuspected. Happy shall we be when that hymn is revealed to us for all eternity and our very life becomes part of it. Then indeed we will know that we have not labored in vain.

The Lamb is on the mountain, at the highest point of the earth, whereas the beast is on the seashore, the lowest point of land. As the mountain is solid so is the seashore slippery. Good must eventually triumph over evil in the world because good is built on the solid foundation of God whereas evil stands on the shaky ground of uncertainty, brute force and, ultimately, chaos.

The hundred and forty-four thousand are virginal, that is, they have not prostituted themselves to idolatry but have remained faithful to their Lord who is their eternal spouse. They have been ransomed from the sufferings of life and from slavery to the power of evil in the world, and they have been ransomed to freedom under God, to the ability to turn all things to good and make their life fruitful for all eternity.

14:6-7

The fifth sign consists of three angelic proclamations that announce for us the final judgment on humanity. The first angel praises God the judge, the second announces the end of evil and the third warns all people to choose wisely and to remain on the side of God. An answering voice from heaven will declare a beatitude in favor of those who have remained just.

Ought we to rejoice in the fact that God sits in judgment when we are not sure how, in our case, that judgment will go? The answer to that is definitely yes because, if judgment is inevitable, there is none who could judge us with as much clemency as God, not even ourselves. In this life, we do encounter many judgments—the judgment of the world, of the people around us, often of our own family, and, possibly worst of all, the judgment that we render against ourselves because we have not achieved the perfection we have hungered for. That self-judgment is usually goaded by pride and therefore is perhaps the least fair of all. Since we are in fact being judged at all stages of our life, it is inevitable, and most desirable, that we should submit to the judgment of God since that judgment alone will scrutinize us in complete fairness and vindicate us when we have been judged harshly and unfairly. I could not even really know who I am if I did not receive the judgment of God over my life.

14:8

The second angel announces the fall of evil and specifically of worldly power which so often tries to enslave us to its whims and turn us from God. The power of the world has its own theology which can be misleading. Who has not heard about patriotism, obedience to rulers, following all laws no matter what? That these can be good things is undisputed. But often they can become the cloak under which worldly power hides its own ambition and arrogance, and then they become the intoxicating wine of propaganda. Government authority would have us believe that even God must submit to its laws, and therein is the danger. Too many crimes have been committed in the world because we assumed that God was the servant (or at least the accomplice) of worldly powers.

14:9–12

The third angel gives us a warning against making wrong choices. Lust, pride, greed, hatred are choices against God, and they bring us an experience of the divine wrath, that sense of alienation that is ours when we know we are not living the way we ought to be. The problem with evil is that it does not fit. It promises great happiness but can only deliver frustration, self-disgust and alienation from others. The symbol of this inner bankruptcy is the burning sulphur that is the punishment of sinners in this ominous passage. The fire, I believe, is the fire of frustration and self-hatred that will burn in sinners when they gaze on heaven— the angels and the Lamb—and realize what their stupidity and their selfishness have robbed them of. To realize that we have lost out on happiness by our own choice has to be one of the most awful feelings in life.

Why do we let ourselves in for such chaos? Shallowness of views, an unwillingness to trust the promises of God or to wait for their fulfillment, belief in the lies of worldly enticements, cause us to grasp for the short-term pleasures rather than work for lasting happiness. Sin promises instant gratification but only hurls us into a downward spiral of greater and greater need for selfish gratifications which give less and less pleasure, the more they are experienced. We become trapped in our own carnal appetites until, sometimes, we come to the point of not even wanting goodness anymore. That may be the point where we choose damnation over salvation, when we destroy our own inner hunger for the divine.

If, then, we die without turning back (conversion) from this path of self-centeredness and sin, we may find ourselves eternally locked into a pattern that we no longer have the will to break, hungering for gratifications that never gratify, seeking ravenously after pleasures that no longer please. The passions we thought were our servants have become our masters and there is no escape. That is damnation, all the more horrible when we realize what could have been and are aware that we would now be incapable of enjoying heaven even if God were to give it to us. Heaven and hell are choices we make while still in this life, choices we must then live with for all eternity since they have become part of us.

14:13

We now come to the sixth sign which consists of three angelic voices pronouncing the blessedness of the just and the final harvest of the earth, now ready to enter into its eternal destiny. The first angelic voice calls forth a beatitude, the second of seven beatitudes that will be pronounced in this book. There is a responding voice, the Spirit's, which assures the just that the merits of their good works will become their eternal inheritance. Since it is the task of the Spirit to build up the church, it is not surprising that the Spirit should place a great deal of emphasis on the good works we accomplish under his inspiration. Our good works are really the only luggage we take with us into heaven.

Happy indeed are the dead who die in the Lord! They never again need to fear that they might offend God and inherit punishment, that they might lose their relationship with him and end up in damnation. All the passions are now under control. There is no more sin to fear, no more frustration to struggle against, no more restlessness or dissatisfaction such as we find in this life. The great gift of God to us is that, in death, we find eternal fulfillment, eternal peace and eternal safety.

14:14–16

The harvest of the earth begins with the harvest of wheat for the making of bread and then goes on to the harvest of the grapes for the making of wine. Hence, in the final harvest, we find a heavily eucharistic message which will be most clear in the harvest of the grapes with its symbol of an abundance of blood.

Perhaps the most consoling thought for me in this harvest symbol is that all life is harvested by God when it is ripe and not before. If we do not make our life fruitful, it is because we have not tried enough, not because God "cut us down" too soon. We are given plenty of time, plenty of opportunities, plenty of graces. The more fruitful we make our life, the more we will be food (bread) for others, the more we will feed their spiritual hunger. As we partake of the bread of life, we become bread of life for others. When we have spoken our word to the world, when we have fed it with the bread of our holiness, we are ready for the final harvest and the eternal reward. Who other than God can ever say whether one has died too soon or lived too long? The One who has the master plan is the only one capable of testing the ripeness of the harvest. Willingly or unwillingly, we must ultimately abandon ourselves to his decision. How lucky we are if we can do so with the realization that his time is the right time, the best time, the most fitting time of all.

14:17-20

The third angelic voice calls for the harvest of the grapes. It is significant that this voice belongs to the angel at the altar of incense. This is the angel whose task it is to offer up the prayers of the saints and therefore who is in charge of the merits of the martyrs. He is the one who offers up the blood of the martyred Christ with which is mingled the blood of all who have been martyred for love of him. This angel knows when the grapes are ripe, when there is sufficient blood for the cleansing of all the sins of humanity. Therefore it is his task to announce when the harvest may begin.

The grapes are tossed into the winepress of God's wrath. This winepress, which is situated outside of the city (on Calvary outside of Jerusalem) is the cross of Jesus on which the grapes of his life were pressed by his suffering and death to release his redeeming blood and thus atone for the sins of humanity which have aroused the outraged wrath of the just God against human injustice. When the blood of Jesus has washed us clean, when we have applied his redemptive grace to our life through our union with him, then we are ready for the harvest, we are ready for heaven.

The fact that there is much blood is not a fearful sight but a joyful one. It means that there is an overabundance of merits in Jesus' crucifixion—more than enough to bring into redemption all who have placed their trust in Jesus and have accepted him as their Lord. No one ever needs to be left out who truly wants to enter; there is enough blood to wash everyone clean and bring all to the realm of eternal justice, to the loving arms of God.

15:1-4

The redeemed of God, those who have not sold out to worldly values, stand on a sea of glass, a symbol of the clarity of vision that they have arrived at through their purity of heart and possibly the counterpart of the sea of chaos on which stand the doers of evil. The world, with its allurements, is transparent to them now; they can see evil for what it is and so they can praise God with joyous hearts because they have resisted the temptation to give in to human greed. They have let go of all those false human values— the mark of the beast—by which the world sought to entice them and they have given their all to the service of God. They have nothing further to fear.

In the song of the redeemed, God is praised for his works, his ways and his deeds. The works of God comprise all of creation and they are indeed mighty and wonderful. Whoever has been in the midst of a storm or on the sea or on a mountain or simply in the presence of a sunrise or a sunset can well exclaim with the redeemed that the works of God are both mighty and wonderful. From the immense outlay of the stars (God's mighty works) to the tiny atom (God's wonderful works), all of creation is an ongoing praise of its creator. In praising God as creator, we are directing our praise specifically to God the Father, the one through whom life originates.

God's ways, his relationship with humanity, are righteous and true. God never deals with us in an unkind way or in a deceitful way. All that he does is done for our greater good and in view of our eternal happiness. The kindness and the graciousness of God are indeed marvelous. To be convinced of that is to enter the way of peace, the way of the redeemed. In praising the ways of God, we are praising his righteousness and his spoken truth and therefore we are directing our praise at God as the Son, the redeemer, the revealer of the divine truth and the visible image of the divine righteousness.

God's deeds, his handling of human history and of our own individual history, are clearly seen (the sea of glass); they are transparent to all those who love God. The only ones who do not see are those who have a vested interest in not seeing. We need only to look back into our life to see how well God has worked in us. Nothing was ever without purpose and everything helped to fashion us into the kind of people God has created us to be. There is no waste in the experiences of life; all have value and all contribute to the development of our personality. This praise of the deeds of God in our life is the praise of his ability to make us holy, and therefore here we are directing our praise to God the Holy Spirit, the sanctifier of the church. The great praise of God in Revelation 15 is therefore truly a trinitarian praise.

This is the song of the redeemed: God's creation is beautiful, he is just and true and his actions are always life-giving for us. God is the perfect community who calls us into an eternal celebration of community. Here is a song well worth singing, and sad indeed is the fate of those who are not capable of singing it. The only ones who can stand on the sea of glass are those who can see clearly the magnificence of God and the perfection of his activities among us.

15:5–8

The seventh sign of this cycle prepares the way for the next cycle, the cycle of the seven bowls, the cycle which mirrors the plagues of Egypt, the punishment of God against a people who refused to accept his will. Since the plagues are nature-oriented, the living creature, symbol of the world, is the possessor of this punishment and it is he who passes it on to the avenging angels.

Nature is on the side of God and will ultimately accomplish the will of God.

The wrath of God, as I see it, is the divine impatience to have me perfect. The smoke which hides the presence of God is a favorite biblical symbol that has a special meaning here. God cannot be seen clearly until his full justice has been meted out to the world. God is revealed by his actions. In that same vein, God's will for me is never fully revealed in my life until that life is complete, until it has slipped into eternity. As long as I am living, I am still subject to being surprised by God. There is a very special thrill for me in that revelation.

8

FIFTH CYCLE—THE BOWLS: REVELATION 16

This short cycle is undoubtedly the most gloomy and negative of the book, and for good reason. It is the punishment that is meted out for sin, a reminder to us of what we can eventually expect if the choices we make in our life are improper choices.

Using imagery from the book of Exodus, the writer warns us of the terrible trap we can fall into if we listen to the voices of the dragon's ominous emissaries. For the first time, we are being introduced to the false prophet, a sign of religion at the service of control and greed. It is not surprising that, after mentioning this personage, the author thunders: "Be on your guard" (16:15). It is easy for us to do nothing and allow negative and dangerous philosophies to take control of our world and of our lives.

In a crescendo of thunder, lightning, and earthquake, the cycle closes on a vision of what can be expected if we choose the wrong values. We now have a clear picture of the danger. Next we will be shown the judgment of God in action upon sinful humanity.

PART 9—FIFTH CYCLE: THE BOWLS

16:1-2

The fifth cycle is a counterpart to the third cycle and, like the trumpets, the bowl represents the inevitable punishment incurred by sin. This is the shortest of the cycles and the only one that does not contain any good news, even in the interlude. After all, what good news could we hope to find in sin? The cycle re-enacts the plagues of Egypt, the classic punishment for evil, and begins with a reminder that the punishment is for those who have accepted the mark of the beast on their body. It is not surprising, therefore, that the first punishment announced is that which afflicts the body. As Saint Paul tells us, "The wages of sin is death." The sinful habits we surrender ourselves to will bring about their own brand of punishment. The list is long: too much smoking may lead to emphysema or lung cancer, too much drinking can usher in sclerosis of the liver, indiscriminate sexual habits can bring venereal diseases, careless driving can cause accidents, tensions, worries and anger can bring about ulcers, and so on. The body will inevitably be threatened and harmed by the negative habits we indulge in.

Not all illness is caused by sin, obviously, but a goodly amount of it is. Often, when sickness strikes, we must say a remorseful "mea culpa." To ask God to take away from us the results of our sinfulness can be an exercise in futility. Our God-given freedom allows us to choose sin if we want to but of necessity obligates us to accept its negative consequences. With freedom comes responsibility and, if we choose foolishly, retribution.

16:3-4

These two bowls belong together since they mention a common catastrophe—blood in the sea and in the rivers. This is a chilling prophecy. Blood, the symbol of life, has become the bringer of death. Sin has turned life symbols into death symbols. The atom, the basic element of life, has become the threat of worldwide death. Human birth, another powerful symbol of life, has, in many instances, been turned into the negation of life called abortion. When our life symbols become death symbols, we have indeed fallen under the shadow of cosmic catastrophe.

If we do not live in the love and peace of God, if we have incurred his wrath through lives of sin, everything we touch seems to turn into the blood of the corpse, the life symbol that begets death. We are created for God and we really cannot make it without him.

16:5-7

The praise of God's judgment here is given in ladder parallelism. God is just in passing sentence, God's sentence is just, and all of God's judgments are true and just.

When we talk about what people deserve, perhaps we ought rather to be talking about what they need. If people's lives are in a drastic way, they may need drastic measures to awaken them to the realization of their folly. The justice of God is manifest in the fact that he gives to all of us what we need in order to repent and be saved. If we reject that gift, the loss is ours. Also ours will be the even greater measures God may have to take with us later in order to bring us to our senses.

The justice of God impels him to seek our conversion because he knows what we stand to gain and to lose and, truth often hard to fathom, he loves us perfectly and never stops loving us, even when we are least deserving of that love. Ah the terrible love of God that will not allow us to find peace in our sin! How angry and bitter that can make us when we do not want to give up sinfulness! There are realistically only two things we can do about the awesome love of God; we can run away from it and face misery, frustration, and anger, or we can run toward it, give up everything that keeps us from him, and find eternal happiness. It is amazing how often we choose the first way and waste years trying to escape the inescapable pursuit of the Eternal Lover.

16:8-11

The scorching of the sun is for us a chilling reminder of the threat of nuclear catastrophe whereas the darkness that follows is akin to the nuclear winter that would inevitably follow such a catastrophe.

Bowl four speaks to us of the pain that comes during the day, the burning pain of heat, and bowl five speaks of its counterpart, the pain of the night, the numbing pain of cold. The sun speaks of the heat of passion and the night speaks of the cold of fear, two great burdens of our human race.

Pain in the day and pain in the night! There is no escape from the torments of a troubled conscience, especially when we will not acknowledge that inner lack of harmony and choose instead to put the blame outside of ourselves. It is because the sun is too hot that we are ill, it is because the night is too deep that we are afraid; all of that provides excuses not to look at the alienation within, the broken bond with God that cries for reconciliation.

The more we blaspheme—put the blame on God—the less we can heal and find inner peace. Is it our pride that will not allow us to take the blame to ourselves or is it the fear that perhaps God is not a loving God and will not help? Pride (the sun) gives us pain and fear (the night) brings us terror. How hard it is to get God to do things our way! Yet God helps us in the way that is most appropriate—not to reassure our vacillating faith, not to boost our greedy ego, not to free us from the pain that calls us to growth or to give us power over others, but in the way which is the most liberating for us. Yet how easily we can come to the point of wanting no help from God except the help we have ourselves chosen and which, if it comes, will prove to us that we have some power over what God will do in our life, that we are the ones in control and that our God is our servant and not our master. It is no wonder that the world should blaspheme when the God it seeks with such insistence is only a figment of its own need for domination and for security and bears no real resemblance to the God who really is.

The final thought, and not a surprising one really, is that the people did not turn away from their wicked deeds. Like all of us, they wanted a God who gave them what they wished (the beast), not a God who demanded integrity and holiness in return (the Lamb).

16:12–16

The sixth bowl is the bowl of war, the inevitable result of not having heeded the symptoms of the first five bowls. Here, the trinity of evil comes into its own, spouting out devils of hatred, of greed, and of suspicion. The dragon (devil image) leads people into immorality, self-centeredness, and a frenzied search for pleasure. That brings us to the realm of the beast, worldly power, the greed of unrestrained capitalism, hunger for the accumulation of possessions. The third member of this anti-trinity now takes over and paves the way to disaster. It is the false prophet, atheism and all the false ideologies that seek to dull the human conscience and convince each nation that it, and it alone, is in the right. It is not surprising that the result of buying into the deceptions of this sinister trinity should be war, violence and worldwide discord.

The seer is giving us an insight into what he discerns is really going on and asking us to be ready for an onslaught against our most precious values. The world has its ways and they are not necessarily God's ways. Trouble is brewing. There is no room for complacency. If we're lying naked in our bed (figuratively), we'll get caught with our pants down (still figuratively) and won't we look silly, we the Christians who were supposed to show the world how one ought to live in order to be happy and at peace!

Often we can look at the gathering clouds and, not really reading the signs of the times, go along with the voice of pride, of greed and of prejudice, calling it patriotism or manliness or some other nonsense. How long Christianity has been lolling naked in its bed when it ought to have been preparing itself an armor of love, of integrity, of justice, of self-discipline, of prayer and of sacrifice! The world, in its search for happiness, depended on our wisdom and our holiness, and all we have given the world is our comfortable snoring, while others, pretending to represent the Christ, have sown hatred, racism, greed and all the frogs of evil that the mouth of the devil and his minions could spew out.

Now there is urgency. Perhaps already the shadows of evening are beginning to gather. The time for sleeping is over. Now it is win on the side of the Lamb or lose to the power of the beast. Now we have to decide for God, strap on our armor, make sure we are fully clothed with that garment of charity which alone can bring us into the heavenly realm. Sleeping is tantamount to being on the side of the enemy since it offers him no resistance and offers the world no viable alternative to his lies. We must wake up. We must offer an enlightened challenge to the pretensions of the spirit of worldliness that one man, one race, one power is better than the others and more worthy to direct the destinies of humankind. There is no voice really worth listening to but that of God. Let us not be timid in saying so to the world.

16:17–21

The seventh cycle of the bowls begins with an ominous statement which has a familiar ring in Christian thought: "It is finished!" (see Jn 19:30). The bowls are drained, the cycles of punishment have been completed. On the cross, Jesus announced that the work of redemption was finished. Now, from the throne of God, there comes the announcement that the spreading of the gospel is finished. The world has been given the message of God's love and the world has responded with Armageddon, a determined decision to fight God, to go its own way, to reject all divine control. Once again the sin of Adam has triumphed in humanity, but this time it can no longer be excused; humanity knows better.

The seventh bowl is poured out on the air and that unleashes the final punishment. When humanity pollutes the air, it has directly affronted the creative Spirit of God, his Ruah; it has damaged the very cycle of creation in the world and tragedy will inevitably ensue. Indeed, what hope is there for us if we pollute the very air we breathe? But there is a deeper meaning here. In the spiritual order, there is also an element of air pollution. When human greed, human sin and human hatred destroy the desire for God in the world, they have fouled up our spiritual air and have damaged our ability to make the leap from the world of the flesh to the world of the spirit, that tremendous leap that Jesus initiated for all of us when he became a man. Our Lord opened the way to the spiritual realm. Modern cynicism, greed and atheism are striving to block that way. The result of that effort is the final bowl, the last cycle of punishment that opens the way to the final struggle between good and evil, the concentration of the forces of the world against the forces of God at Armageddon. When the Spirit of God is disregarded in the world, there is nothing left for humanity but punishment.

The defiling of the creative Ruah of God is the final symbol of humanity's failed stewardship. The ancient covenant of God with humanity and all creation (Gen 9:12) has been broken when humanity fails to keep its part of it and to live within the sacred trust of its stewardship. The result is the unleashing of nature's forces against a betraying humanity. Three forms of punishment result from the polluting of God's Ruah—lightning and thunder, earth-quake, and a hailstorm. These have a symbolism which, although rooted in nature, has a meaning deeper than nature and extend-ing into the very core of the human reality.

The lightning and thunder, symbol of an angry avenging nature, is the unleashing against humanity of the forces from above, the sky's response to humanity's failed stewardship. Its deeper meaning hints at human rage which calls down a respond-ing rage. The earthquake is the unleashing against humanity of the forces from below, the earth's response to humanity's failed stewardship. It can also symbolize human violence which calls up a responding violence from the very core of the earth. Human hatred and violence have turned all of creation against its un-faithful lords. The third punishment, the hailstones, the bom-bardment of the earth, possibly represents the sins of humanity falling back on humanity to plague it and deepen its sufferings. All the negatives which we spill out, anger, violence and sin, now fall back on us in a terrible reckoning. It is inevitable that, sooner or later, we reap the harvest of our own inner lack of harmony. Inner chaos calls forth outer chaos. Sins don't simply remain a personal reality; they also afflict all with whom we come into con-tact. Angry people are destructive people, selfish people are un-just people, those who surrender to sinful habits tend to use other people. Sinfulness is never just a matter of "my own life and my right to live it as I want"; there are always repercussions on others, and hence it is always reprehensible to God, the loving Father who calls us to live in loving harmony with each other and with all of creation. When the measure of sin overflows, the world is caught up in its malevolence, all life suffers, and therefore God must act.

Since the problem affects the whole world, the result will be presented in terms of four consequences, four being of course the numerical symbol for the world. The first result of the rampaging of evil is that the cities are split apart. Civil war, crime, violence within are results of human selfishness and insensitivity. Sin separates us into classes, ethnic groups, social privileges. There is in humanity an innate clannishness that selfishness stirs up to the surface with disastrous results in terms of social upheaval. The more we live in sin, the more we are split apart, the more fragmented becomes our humanity.

The wine of wrath is offered to the offending human race. Selfishness breeds injustice and injustice breeds hatred which in turn breeds crime and violence, resulting in greater and more grievous injustices. When people are threatened, they become more defensive, they become entrenched in the prejudices that caused the problems in the first place, and nothing is solved. The wine of wrath is what inevitably results when the fabric of society is torn by self-centeredness and prejudice. Peace will forever evade us unless we are willing to re-establish justice.

As society becomes more and more entrenched in selfishness, the islands flee; communication between countries begins to break down more and more. Fear and suspicion replace trust and the world becomes an armed camp. Then we have terrorism, massacres, conflicts, and all sorts of international hatred as vested-interest groups jockey for positions of prestige and of power without regard for the rights of others.

The next consequence of evil is the gradual loss of our ethical values. The mountains, symbol of our prayer life and our connectedness with God, disappear. A "me-first" attitude replaces patriotism and selfless service to others. Money and power are the bottom line in human interactions, and so it should not be surprising that trust disappears. This is the most terrible consequence of humanity's failed stewardship, this breakoff of the spiritual connection. When opportunism replaces idealism, there is little to connect us to our God. We lose our relationship with him and we can easily slip into blasphemy, that is, into blaming God for the sufferings that we have received as a result of our own sinfulness. It is a sad reality that, when things go bad for us, we are prone to put the blame on God. Then we rage against God for the sicknesses we have brought on ourselves, the accidents that our carelessness has caused, the misbehavior of the children we have failed to raise properly. When we close the door on God through our anger, where else is there for us to go? Then we have set the stage for the sights, the final struggle between good and evil in the world. We are either for God or we are against him. At Armageddon, no one remains neutral.

9

SIXTH CYCLE—THE SIGHTS: REVELATION 17, 18, 19 AND 20

This cycle is one of the most important of the book. It outlines for us the resolution of the conflict between the two ideologies that have been battling for control of humankind. Babylon (oppressive power and self-serving wealth) is unmasked and defeated. No power on earth can equal the power of goodness. There is in all of us an innate hunger to do what is right and good that nothing can ever defeat. As the two witnesses of chapter 11, our hunger for the divine will always return to life, no matter how hard we try to ignore it or to crush it. God the creator has placed in each of us an in-built movement toward him that is one of the most fundamental qualities of the human person.

The cycle begins with a long reflection on the unmasking and fall of the harlot which represents power and greed. Four classes of people mourn over her loss and four classes rejoice over it. Then the author gives us a sevenfold outline of what can destroy the fabric of a nation.

Joyful praise and celebration breaks forth in heaven over the failure of human sinfulness, and in it we are given an introduction to an image that will become central in the next cycle, the bride of Christ.

The cosmic Christ now comes forth for the final confrontation with evil. After a reflection on the impact of the servants of the Lamb upon the world, we will be shown the final scene, the resolution of the struggle, the triumph of God in our world and in our own individual hearts. We have looked at the whole panorama of the human conflict; we are ready for the final cycle, the

Christian ideal that has been entrusted to us and that will bring us
rejoicing into the arms of God.

PART 10—SIXTH CYCLE: THE FIRST TWO SIGHTS

17:1-6a

Out of the seventh bowl comes the next cycle, the cycle of the
sights. Here we come to the resolution of the ideological struggle
between the Lamb of God and Satan. The first image that is
introduced to us is the counterpart of the holy mother, the harlot.
As the holy mother begets children of integrity for the service of
God, so the harlot begets children of evil for the service of Satan.
As the holy mother was standing in glory, the harlot is sitting in
desolation. One wears the gold of the sun, the other the scarlet of
evil. Once again, in this cycle, the seer deals with the powerful
imagery of contrasts.

The harlot is seated on the scarlet beast of worldly power, and
she is a harlot because she is causing the people of God to become
unfaithful to their divine spouse, the Lamb. Most vulnerable to
her enticements are the kings, the rulers of countries, who so often
choose the pursuit of power over the pursuit of holiness. The
harlot is drunk. She has what she sees as a winning combination.
Power holds the key to wealth and therefore can control people
through their pocketbooks. Not too many people, unfortunately,
are all that willing to suffer for the sake of holiness, as Jesus put
it (Mt 5:10). What is profitable tends to be far more enticing
than what is ethical. There is not much money to be made out
of holiness.

For all her trappings, the harlot is in a desolate place. No
matter how enticing wealth and power may be, they are no sub-
stitutes for the inner peace and harmony (the shalom) of a good
life which alone brings real happiness. Wherever God is not, there
is always desolation. Power, as many a ruler has found, is a lonely
place to be, a place where one has few friends one can really trust,
a place where there is little true community and little sincere love.
The price of wealth and power is often personal isolation even
amidst the cheers of the crowds.

The beast we encounter here is the beast of chapter 13 which blasphemously passes itself off for God. The beast of human power-structures claims either to speak for God (capitalism) or to be God (communism). Either way, its voice is the voice of blasphemy, seeking to lead people astray for the sake of its own security, claiming that where there is power and wealth there is God. The beast has seven heads; it has all human knowledge at its disposal and great cleverness in getting its own way. It has ten horns, again the echo of the ten general persecutions against the church and the ten emperors who initiated them. Rulers may presume divine powers for themselves, but they come and go quickly enough and none of them ever maintain themselves more than a very short time. What is the short-lived arrogance of human power in the face of divine eternity?

Coming back to the harlot, we are told that she is dressed in purple, symbol of imperial power (government by arrogance), and in scarlet, symbol of military strength (government by terror). The trappings of tyrants do not change much over the centuries. As nations tend to be, so, very often, do individuals. Who of us is not at times tempted to get our own way by arrogance (the know-it-all attitude) or by ruthlessness (the bullying tactics)? Governments, for better or for worse, reflect the mood of their own citizens. The harlot wears gold and pearls, products of land and sea and symbol of the wealth that is at the disposal of governments, especially self-serving governments. Wealth, as we saw in chapter 13, is at the service of power and vice versa. They are the necessary, if not always liberating, elements of the social reality.

Another contrast is offered us in this sight; the cup of lewdness which stands in opposition to the cup of God's wrath. The cup of lewdness defiles people; the cup of wrath cleanses them. The cup of lewdness makes people drunk, unable to judge properly between right and wrong; the cup of wrath sobers people up, forces them to see the consequences of a negative way of life. Certainly the cup of lewdness is by far the most enticing to people. It makes few demands and gives much pleasure but, like an overindulgence in wine, it leaves only a bad headache.

The symbolic name on the forehead of the harlot is hardly a

complimentary one, and it is unlikely that the harlot is fond of having it deciphered. No matter how well we cover up our hunger for power and wealth, sooner or later our forehead, our attitude, reveals who and what we really are. There is no way we can go on fooling people. When the look on the face denies the honey of the spoken words, people are quick to realize they are being lied to. As befits a servant of the trinity of evil, the harlot's name has three attributes. She is Babylon, that sinister symbol of evil empire bent on subjugating everyone to its will. No matter how well conquerors try to justify their actions, the pride of power and greed remains evident, especially to their victims. The second part of the name is mother of harlots. The harlot has a way of corrupting all social systems sooner or later. As power succeeds, others seek to seize power. As wealth succeeds, others grasp after wealth. Little wonder there is no real peace in the world. The third part of the harlot's name is mother of the world's abominations. Here she is identified with the gruesome idols of the nations whose purpose was so often to rationalize the evil lives of people (Zeus the womanizer, Mercury the thief, Venus the nymphomaniac, etc.) rather than call them to sensible ethical values. One of the favorite maneuvers of wealth and power is to warp ethical values in order to justify its own conduct. Repression becomes the safety of the state, empire-building is called civilizing other nations, war is called the building up of a lasting peace. The excuses are many and they can make people "drunk" for a while, but eventually people sober up and the games of the manipulators of life are uncovered.

Once again the harlot is said to be drunk, and this time there is an even more ominous quality to her drunkenness. She has persecuted the people of God and the persecution seems to have worked, to have been successful. Perhaps that is the most dangerous drunkenness of all, this assumption that persecution can successfully remove opposition to power. When governments begin to persecute those of their citizens who stand for the ethical values of the country, the governments are truly in trouble. The memory of the martyr stands as the strongest opposition to the repressiveness of governments. There are none more alive and more powerful to effect change than those who have died for their beliefs.

17:6b–8

The prophet is astonished and the sinners are amazed at the sight of the beast that the harlot is riding on. The two words used here are for all intents and purposes synonymous. In other words, the feeling aroused by the beast is similar in both but with very different results. Astonishment is a matter of being stricken with fear whereas amazement is more along the lines of bewildered wonder. Both words could be used almost interchangeably. What leads one to fear leads the other to fascination. The difference resides not in the sight itself but in the disposition of the one doing the seeing. If the "men of the earth" had had their names written in the book of life, they would have been astonished (afraid of the evil), not amazed (drawn to it). What is life for one is death for the other. It is all a matter of what is in the heart.

What is the beast that once was dead and has come back to life? What it was, in the narrow context of John's understanding, is less important than what it is in the broader context of human history. The beast of the Roman empire, I believe, was the domination of the state over faith values, what one might call atheistic paganism. Rome professed belief in a multitude of gods but obeyed no God other than its own power. That concept of a religion of convenience died with the Christianization of Rome but soon came back to life again, especially since the enlightenment period when the power of the state became all important again. The new atheism is not much different from that of Rome; religious beliefs must conform to the state's will or face persecution, overt or covert. The methods may be more civilized (generally) but the intent has not changed a great deal; the welfare of the state is still seen as more important than the ethical values of its people.

17:9–14

The seer now gives us four clues to the understanding of his rather complex message. The beast has seven heads which are also seven hills. The head, of course, represents knowledge, scientific knowledge at the service of rulers, and the hills in this context are a symbol of human pride and arrogance which in this case is seen as complete (the number seven), that is, without limits. It is a sad fact that, once we have chosen evil, we may soon lose all ability to limit the evil; it begins to overpower us. After a while, anything is seen as permissible if it will benefit the one who has chosen to walk along that self-serving path. Knowledge and pride at the service of individual ambition—it can be an ominous alliance as we have seen only too well in this century. One only has to call to mind Hitler, Stalin, Pol Pot and, sadly, many others, not to mention the less successful but no less terrible mass murderers who spring up in our own country from time to time.

The second clue is seven kings, a dynasty in full (not seven as a number but as a sign of fullness). Perhaps what we are seeing here is a way of governing that is going out of style; the whole concept of the personality cult (speaking of the state as "Caesar," the man in charge). That leads us to the third clue, the resurrected Nero—the false resurrection as opposed to the true resurrection of Christ. The personality cult will disappear for a while but will be resurrected and will have a short return to popularity. The divine emperors that the seer knew about will be replaced by the man-of-all-answers, the modern Hitlers and their likes. Even more than that, the resurrected personality cult points to the antichrist, the personal opposite to the Christ, who perhaps is yet to come.

The fourth clue speaks of ten kings who will reign for only an hour. In the short context, this reminds us of the two hundred years of in-fighting that Rome was about to experience, a time when emperors came and went at a very rapid rate, few of them staying in power for any length of time. There is also a deeper meaning to the clue, I believe, and it is that a new form of power will be established, a power resting in the state itself rather than in its leaders. The ten kings give their authority over to the beast (the state) and become its servants. The phenomenon is easily recognizable in our modern governmental structures, for better or for worse.

All these power structures ultimately seem to come into conflict with the Lamb who represents the only legitimate personality cult the world has ever known because he is the only personality that is completely life-giving to others. One thing the seer is sure of, however, is that the Lamb will win; ethical values are long-lasting, holiness works and ultimately conquers all opposition.

There is no power on earth that equals the power of the saints, those chosen (called specifically by God for his service) and faithful (living their calling with honesty and courage).

A personal application might be made of this passage, I believe. The closer we come to the Lord, the more we are likely to be tempted, the more we can become a threat to the evil influences (demonic) of the world. With this greater danger there is also a greater power because, as we come closer to the Lamb, we tap into the Lamb's own power more and more and we ourselves are empowered to face and overcome all opposition. The battle does not end because we are closer to God; it continues on a higher level and with higher stakes. But we can be confident; the Lamb, as Saint John tells us, has overcome the world (Jn 16:33).

17:15–18

Evil cannot thrive except inasmuch as people allow it to. We choose the rule of evil; it is not imposed on us. That is something we need to remember. Evil may be out there but it will not enter our lives unless we invite it in, unless, like the harlot, we find it desirable.

Evil is destroyed by its children, what it has begotten. So it is in our lives; we come to a point where we see evil for what it is and turn against it. The power of sin may hold us enslaved but it cannot keep us blind to its evil forever. With God's help, we will always find the courage to turn against it, to strip it of its fineries, its appealing lies, and remove it from our lives.

The ten horns turn from the harlot (worldly power) to the beast (false religiosity). Often a person turns from a life of sin only to fall into spiritual rigidity and a blisteringly judgmental attitude. True religion is loving acceptance, false religion is bigotry and harshness in the name of God.

18:1–3

The terrible price of sin: Babylon (the person given over to sin) has become a cage for evil spirits (anger, bitterness, disillusionment, the inability to forgive or let go of a hurt) and for filthy birds (sinful habits: lust, alcoholism, over-eating, all the physical excesses that plague us). A cage is that which imprisons, will not let out or allow to go free. It is chilling to think that Babylon will not let go of the evil. Does there come a time in our life when the evil we have clung to is all we have left, when we fear to let go of it because then our life would be empty, deserted? An example that comes to mind is a married couple who hate each other, who make each other miserable, and yet will not let go of each other for fear of having nothing left if they do.

How terrible it is to think that we could come to a point where evil is all we have left and we must cling to it with bitter determination for fear of having nothing, of being completely naked against the world. Well can the seer say at this point, "Alas, Babylon!" This is an apt warning to humanity to choose good and not evil, lest eventually we should become possessed by evil.

18:4-8

The warning to God's people is to stay away from the cage in which Babylon is trapping herself. If we do not avoid the pitfalls, we will be trapped, as so many others are trapped, by the two snares mentioned at the start of this chapter, excusing our sinfulness and blindly following after pleasures. These negative elements are destructive to our personality and even to our physical life. Undisciplined living destroys the body and so can anger and hatred, the open invitations to ulcers, high blood pressure and heart attack. We have also seen of late how damaging indiscriminate sexual pleasure can be. To that, we may add the damage to our credibility and our reputation done by lies and deceitful conduct. Negative behavior carries its own punishment and, if we want to avoid that punishment (the plagues), we had better depart from the negative behavior and not let ourselves be fooled by the voices that promise bliss and deliver only misery. The slogans are all around us: "It's foolish to deny yourself." "If it feels good, do it." "Don't get mad, get even." The boasts of Babylon are many and, if unchecked, they will eventually lead to its downfall.

It is difficult sometimes for us not to get caught up in the spirit of worldliness that so often prevails around us. Self-serving people, no matter what boasts they may make, find no lasting happiness. Beware the boasters! People who are comfortable about their life do not need to boast about it, to try to convince others that they are right. Boasts only cover uneasiness and the suspicion that perhaps one's way is not as right as one would like to think. The people who are always clamoring about how happy they are may not be happy at all. Truly happy people do not need to convince others or themselves of their happiness. It is sufficient for them to experience that happiness and to live in it.

18:9-10

Now begins the dirge of the world, the core of the second sight. There are four groups of mourners, a worldwide symbol. Those who mourn over the destruction of evil are of two kinds—those who stood to benefit from the continuation of the evil and those whose participation in it makes them fearful of a like fate.

The first group of mourners are the kings, the power structures of the world. The breakdown of Rome's power leaves them unprotected and with good reasons to fear retaliations from those they have oppressed. Often the lever of rulers is to create enemies so that the ruler will be seen as a protector from those enemies. The result of power games in the world is far more often divisive than unitive. The only union created is a union of force, a union of fear, and one that will crumble once the power structure loses its backing. The kings have reason to mourn; without the support of Rome, they are at the mercy of their enemies, and since they imitated the ruthlessness of Rome, they can expect the same catastrophe for themselves as has befallen Rome.

18:11-14

The merchants join the dirge because they are losing their market, not because Babylon is afflicted. Here we have the mourning of commercialism, and it is a self-centered mourning. When stability is destroyed, the merchants are likely to be hurt in their pocketbook; hence their reason for supporting any government that enables them to continue making money. Who can tell how many wars have been instigated in the world for the purpose of protecting the market of the merchants? The sad fact is that possibly most wars (if not all) have greed as one of their driving forces. There is, obviously, a need to survive in the world, and each nation has the obligation to protect its economic structure, but this ought not to be done at the expense of other nations, especially of economically poorer nations. There is something wicked about taking advantage of the vulnerability of others.

The triumph of the Christian ideal might not be seen as such good news to the merchant element of the world because of its direct challenge to greed. Not surprisingly, wealth is more often on the side of the church's oppressors than on the side of the church. No wonder the seer sees greed as the mark of the antichrist. Nothing delays the advent of justice in the world more than the fact that, commercially, it is not seen as profitable.

18:15–17a

The next group that comes forward to mourn might have their modern equivalent in the bankers and the money brokers of the world. The stock market is always in a precarious balance when the status quo begins to crumble. The speculators who live and get rich off the money of others are seen here as mourning the internal collapse of the power structure. As Isaiah tells us, there is a web that is woven over all nations (Is 25:7), and the money speculators are a great part of it. At best, it is hard to keep the balance. When one strand is broken somewhere in the world, the whole economic web begins to shake.

Those who have placed their trust in God and not in monetary security are least likely to be deeply affected by any social crisis. Holy simplicity and a firm trust in God allow us to ride through any storm and come out strengthened and better in control of our life.

18:17b–19

The international traders now come forward to mourn. They are an integral part of the web and often the cause of much human misery. From slave trading to setting up corporations in foreign countries and interfering with their internal politics, the international traders have often instigated wars and supported tyranny for the sake of profit. Like all the other children of greed, they need a power base on which to lean or their activities will be hampered, if not actually curtailed. Perhaps these, even more than any others, will need to sing a dirge when the cause of God finally triumphs in the world.

18:20

This is the moment for which the martyrs of chapter 6 have been waiting, the vindication of God's people, the proof that it is God's way that works, not the way of worldly greed.

Just as four groups were called to mourn, four groups are called to rejoice, thus keeping the balance that is so dear to the writer of Revelation. These might be divided into two groups of two: the heavens and the saints, the apostles and the prophets. The first two are general categories; the second two refer specifically to the activities of the church.

The heavens, of course, represent all the spiritual beings who carry out the commands of God and who oversee the activities of humanity. These have cause to rejoice that a major hindrance to their influence is being removed. This first group we might call those who serve on the spiritual level of the cosmic human struggle. The second group is the saints, and these are those who serve on the physical level of the struggle. I see them as a general group because there are saints in all societies and in all religious convictions. The saints, then, are all the holy people in the world, whether Christian or non-Christian, who are trying to accomplish God's will. These have cause to rejoice at the destruction of Babylon, the despoiler of God's plan.

The next two groups mentioned are specifically Christian; they are the apostles and the prophets. The apostles are those who bear witness to Christ—the preachers, the teachers, the inspirers of the church. They are the ones who call all the world to follow Jesus and to abandon sinfulness. They will certainly rejoice at the destruction of a power based on the glorification of sin.

As the saints are the workers on the level of church ethics, the prophets are the workers on the level of economic justice. They are those who speak boldly for God's values and who challenge the injustices in the world. They are the ones who become the martyrs and who, therefore, have the greatest right to call for punishment. The destruction of Babylon will mean the re-establishment of that justice for which they spoke and for which they died. They, most of all, will have cause to rejoice at the destruction of Babylon.

PART 11—SIXTH CYCLE: THIRD TO SIXTH SIGHTS

18:21–24

The millstone that is sinking Babylon is the breakdown of the social order, the loss of civil harmony. Six causes are presented, thus emphasizing the concept of imperfection. When these six causes become evident in a country, that country may be heading for major social problems. Hence, they warrant a closer look.

The stilling of music is the loss of joy in a civilization. When a people gets so caught up in its own importance that it has no place for joy and laughter, there is not much incentive for it to continue. There is little that is more pathetic than a people which has forgotten simple joys and the spirit of celebration.

On the individual level, that loss of joyfulness resultant from our taking ourselves too seriously is also a danger sign. If life becomes too heavy, too serious, we may become a burden to ourselves and to others and we are no longer really in a position to engage in life-giving ministry.

Craftsmen, those who take pride in their work, are one of the special treasures of any healthy civilization. When good craftsmanship is superseded by greed for money, the national pride suffers. What can we say of a culture that puts crafts on a production line and pushes individual craftsmen out of private business? Where is the pride in good work to be found after that? Our country's automation may be the coup de grace to our national pride in good craftsmanship.

All of us are creatures of a creator God and we need to take pride in our work, we need to do well whatever we do. When we begin to do sloppy work, to just put in our time, a great part of our life is wasted. Labor, if it is to be meaningful, must be another way of praising and serving our creator God; otherwise we waste our time and we begin to lose our touch with the divine.

No sound of the mill; the shortage of food is a symptom of the breakdown of a civilization, of the lack of protection toward its farming communities. When we do not sufficiently respect our farmers or when we drive them out of business to replace them with farming corporations, we may begin to lose our identity as a free people and we may become economically enslaved to those corporations. Lack of support for those who produce the nation's food supply is a deadly sign of a country's inner bankruptcy.

As we bring this reflection down to the personal level, we are reminded of the need for proper respect for food in our own individual life. Too much food or too little or an unbalanced diet can affect our spiritual life in very negative ways. If we wish our spirit to flourish, we would be wise not to neglect the health of our body.

The burning lamp is the symbol of scholarly pursuit and of maintaining a high quality of education. A country that neglects its academic community is neglecting the brain capability of its own people and may be dooming itself to scientific stagnation. As our education is, so is our science. No society will long thrive that does not support the proper education and the research activities of its scientists and its intellectuals.

On the personal level, when we no longer wish to study, when we are no longer open to new ideas and fresh ways of looking at life, we become entrenched and we no longer grow. The unwillingness to accept new concepts and to develop new skills dooms individuals as well as nations to a state of stagnation.

The voice of the bridegroom and the bride represents respect for marriage and the family life. When out-of-wedlock children are as numerous as children of a proper marriage, when abortion becomes an acceptable practice, when divorce destroys half of our marriages, we could be heading for a social catastrophe.

When our sexual integration is amiss, we run the risk of developing some uncomfortable personality problems. Sexism, chauvinism, all those attitudes that divide the male and the female and change cooperation into competition, can cause grave damage to our relationships and also to our inner integration. Failure to have proper respect for sexual differences and sexual activities will bring us a loss of personal harmony and the inability to minister fruitfully to others.

In the last verse there is a chilling reminder for us. When we try to control the world's economy, when money-making becomes more important than the freedom and happiness of people, when we bully with money those we cannot bully with force of arms, we have already come under the indictment of God, we have become a new example of Babylon the great, the persecutor of the prophets, of those who voice protests for the abuses, the injustices and the power hunger of the country. It is an ominous sign of moral bankruptcy in a country when it moves against its own spiritual leaders and tries to silence the voice of integrity, the call to maintain life-giving values. Nothing perhaps more clearly points to a social breakdown than this determination to silence the prophets, to dull the national conscience.

On the personal level, we can also move to silence and to persecute the prophets. When we engage in rationalization, when we try to "canonize" our vices and excuse our weaknesses, we are heading for moral bankruptcy. When we can no longer afford to hear the truth about ourselves, we have closed the door to life and to conversion. The more we need to defend ourselves, the more we may be proving that our conduct is indefensible.

19:1-4

As this chapter begins, we find three alleluias and an amen. The three alleluias (Praise God!) are the perfect praise offered to God by the citizens of heaven who admire his infinite integrity and his proper judgment concerning the moral bankruptcy of human greed for wealth and power. The Amen (So be it!) is the wish that such judgment will indeed be carried out whenever human lack of integrity begins to break down the harmony of God's works of salvation.

The twenty-four elders (the faith community) and the four creatures (nature) join in that hymn of praise. It is indeed good to know that God is firmly on the side of truth and justice. It fortifies us in our struggle to retain our own integrity and to continue with unflagging courage the work of our sanctification.

19:5-8

A voice comes from the throne, calling all redeemed humanity to praise God. There is a tremendous sense of equality here. Great and small alike are called to join in the praise; there is no distinction on the level of class or accomplishments; anyone who reveres God deserves to take place in the chorus of praise to God.

Since this passage deals with the praise of God, occasioned by the removal of evil from the world, we are going to deal a lot in threes, the holy number for the divine. To begin with, there are three elements to the roar of praise. It is given by great crowds (all humanity), by the roaring of the deep (the powers below us) and by peals of thunder (the powers above us). Hence, the praise that begins on earth reverberates to its very depths and to its greatest heights. It is hard to imagine a more magnificent description of the praise that is due our God.

Deepening the reflection, we now look at three reasons for that praise, once again resorting to the triune symbol for our triune God. The first praise is to the Lord as king, the second to the Lamb, and the third to the church which is the creation of the Holy Spirit. Hence, in this beautiful hymn, there is reference to Father, Son, and Holy Spirit. It is the complete reality of the divine that we praise, not just some segments of that reality. We cannot afford to make our praise of God too narrow or too limited.

The praise of God with which this hymn begins is itself triune, not surprisingly. In that way, it is truly a trinitarian praise. God is king, that is, he is the ruler of all the world, and this corresponds to the present and also to Jesus who is king of the world. He is God—that is, creator—and in that we have a reference to the past and also, specifically, to the Father. And he is almighty—that is, all that he does succeeds. Here we have a reference to the saving activity of God, what the Hebrew writings call salvation history. This is the specific work of the Holy Spirit, the fashioner of history, of the future. Present, past, future; Son, Father and Spirit; there always needs to be a cosmic scope to the praise of God.

The second part of this hymn of praise centers on Jesus, the Lamb of God, whose wedding day (complete triumph in history) is now being announced. What he has begun in his short lifespan on earth will come to completion at the end of time. The wedding day of the Lamb is the parousia.

The third part of the hymn is assigned to the bride who is the specific work of the Holy Spirit, the sanctifier. The bride is, of course, redeemed humanity, chosen now as the eternal companion of the Lamb, to "follow the Lamb wherever he goes" (Rev 14:4) for all eternity. The bride is adorned with all the virtuous deeds of the saints, the fruits of the Spirit's work in his people. Holiness is the garment that makes us companions of the Lamb, that makes us recognizable as his followers, since in biblical terminology the garment one wears is a symbol of what one's life is all about. The work of God, Father, Son and Spirit, goes on inexorably in the world in spite of any opposition that human greed and selfishness, inspired by the anti-trinity of evil, can place in its way. Central to our praise of God is the realization that, in him, we are firmly on the winning side of life.

19:9-10

The fourth sight ends with the fourth beatitude of Revelation, and this beatitude is pronounced on all those who are privileged to witness the wedding feast of the Lamb, his triumph at the parousia. What follows this beatitude is a reflection on the angelic state. In answer to the prophet's attempt to worship him, the angel announces that he is "merely a fellow servant with you," hence placing himself on an equal footing with the seer. This allows for some conjectures. Are we in fact slated to become another angelic choir at the parousia? Is that why, on the wedding feast of the Lamb, the angel announces equality between him and us?

Those who come to the wedding feast of the Lamb are those who have borne witness to Jesus. To bear witness to Jesus, the seer tells us, is to be a prophetic voice in the world, one who speaks for

God. That is also the calling of the angels—to be messengers for God to the world. Hence that statement of equality with its tremendous promise of glory for the human family.

19:11–16

"Justice is his standard." We need to remember that as we live out our lives. Often we can become comfortable with situations of injustice. The "oh well" response is hardly worthy of the prince of justice. As we are called to be merciful, so are we called to be just. The one ought not to be sacrificed in favor of the other. Faithfulness, truth and justice are necessary components of the Christian life and they should not be watered down. The Lord never said being a Christian was easy; he only said it was wonderful.

In the great battle to which we are led by the Lord, none of our ethical values must ever be sacrificed. To do so would be to become no better than those who war against the Lord. To use the weapons of evil against evil is to become evil. The martyrs of the early church clearly understood that; they chose to die faithful to their ethics. Had they chosen to do otherwise, there might not be a Christianity now for us to champion. We have been given a sacred trust and we must be careful to preserve it entire for the day of the Lord. Christianity is demanding; it calls us to become saints and does not really offer us the option to settle for less.

There are seven names given to Jesus in this passage, and thus they stand for the full reality of his mission and for the perfection of his life. The first name is faithful; Jesus will never abandon us, he will always be part of our life. He who loved us unto death will love us unto eternity. He is true; all that he says must be believed because there is neither falsehood nor deception in him, not even insufficient knowledge. He is just; he will set all things right, he will always be fair to everyone. In fact, justice is his standard, that for which he struggles. That means that if we want to do battle under the standard of the Lord, we also must be people of justice, people who treat everyone fairly. The attributes of the divine Lord must also be the attributes of anyone who has chosen to be his follower.

The fourth name of Jesus is an unknown name, a symbol of the fact that we will never know all about him, that there will always be more to learn, more to discover. It is also symbolic of the fact that he cannot be manipulated by anyone. He cannot be fully named; hence, in biblical thought, he cannot be controlled. Jesus is an eternally free agent who calls us also to live in freedom.

Continuing the revelation of the Lord, he is the word of God, a favorite symbol in Johannine writings. He reveals the Father to us and we can know of God only that which Jesus chooses to reveal. He is King of kings; that is, he has fullness of power, even over the rulers of the earth. Therefore, nothing can happen that is beyond Jesus' power; he can see us through anything. And, finally, he is Lord of lords; he has fullness of authority. He controls the wealth of the world and can give it to whomever he chooses, whomever he sees as having need of it to continue ministry effectively. All of us seek a perfect ruler. Jesus is that ruler, he alone; there is no other that it is fully worth our while to follow.

19:17–21

This vignette about the cosmic battle between good and evil begins with the appearance of an angel so bright it can be seen even with the background of the sun behind it. When God triumphs in the world, there is great clarity, greater than even the sun can bring. He makes sense for us of all the things we puzzled over, the things that have so often hurt us. He lets us see that what we took to be the triumph of evil was only an illusion, darkness by comparison to the real light. The angel of light now announces the dissipation of that darkness and extends an invitation to the birds, the lower species of God's creation, to feed on humanity, God's highest species in this world. No more will the little be oppressed by the great, no more will nature be at the mercy of human greed. It is now time to reverse the roles. As we fed on the other species of the earth, often dooming them to extinction, now they have their revenge. Nature itself triumphs over its unfaithful lord, humanity.

The two beasts of chapter 13 are seen leading the attack against the Lord. The beast of power drags the kings of the earth, its followers, to their doom. The beast of commerce, here called the false prophet, provides the weapons of war through science, industry, wealth. Following this sad group are all those who have bought into their faulty philosophy of what brings happiness, the armies of the kings, the little people of the earth who have let themselves be misled by the empty promises of the great.

The conclusion is foregone and swift. The beasts of power and greed are hurled into the abyss, condemned to an eternal punishment, an eternal burning. They are hurled in alive, that is, fully aware of what has happened to them and why. Unlike them, the unlucky kings and their armies die not really knowing how badly they have been misled. That is the final heartbreak of life— to die never knowing what might have brought us eternal happiness or how easily we might have obtained it, had we set our sights high enough. Perhaps this not knowing is a final act of kindness by a God who only knows how to do what is good and who grieves deeply when any of us rejects the good that he has so generously offered.

20:1–3

The sixth sight is a short one but it is good news for the embattled church. After three hundred years of persecution, the pagan power is to be smashed and the Roman empire will become Christian and begin to build up what it tried for so long to tear down. It is only a breathing spell, and ultimately the devil will be unchained to smash the unity of Christianity and put a new image on the struggle, the fighting of Christian against Christian in the name of Christianity.

How does the devil deceive the nations? I believe he does that the same way he tried to deceive Jesus in the temptation in the desert, by equating power with divinity. The most eminent attribute of God is not power but creativity as the fruit of an all-embracing love. Herein perhaps is the problem. The nations survive on power, not on love, and it is power that they see as the ultimate attribute. Power is far more a need of the devil, however, than the concern of God.

The deception comes when the devil whispers his lies to the

nations: "You are the best nation on earth. Your way is the only way that makes sense. Conquer your neighbor so you can have peace. To listen to the state is to listen to God." The lies are numerous and the word for them is ethnocentrism. There is an unspoken belief in too many people that the nation is in fact God, the one legitimate master of human destiny.

Once a nation has been led astray into believing its own divinity, it must of necessity persecute those who stand as prophets in its midst, those who remind it that there is only one God and that his will, not the will of the state, must prevail. To instigate persecution against the people of God, the devil has only to achieve one thing—convince the state of its divine rights. Then, rapidly, the state slips into a position of being at enmity with God and with those who champion the cause of God which is justice, peace and love.

The only thing that keeps the devil chained is to be faced with a state that follows a greater law than its own. The truly Christian state is the instrument of God for good order in the world. Perhaps one of the things that the devil hates the most is good order.

The deception of the nations is also the deception of the individual. When power, control, domination become our goals, we have put ourselves in the place of God and we are no longer really able to hear him. Then we want a God who obeys us, who gives us power, who condones our domination of others. Like the devil in the gospel of Matthew, we can get into the dangerous position of quoting scripture for our benefit, to show proof that our way, and only our way, is right. When scripture becomes our weapon for domination, we have indeed been deceived by the enemy of our spiritual life.

PART 12—TWO INTERLUDES: THE SEVENTH SIGHT

20:4-6

Between the end of the Roman persecution and the shattering of Christian unity at the reformation, there is roughly a thousand years, so, in that purely historical context, this passage is prophetic. The attack of the devil against the church was a subtle one; he brought it within the power structure of the nations and tricked it into becoming another political power, hence giving it a vested interest in the games of power and greed. Once that was accomplished, the church could no longer stand in judgment over the state; it had lost its ability to be prophetic. The next step was easy; as the church had judged the state, now the state began to judge the church.

However, I see in this passage a far deeper meaning than the mere historical reality, impressive as that may be. There is here a profound reflection on Christian ministry, what is called in this passage "priesthood"—not the cultic reality of ordained priesthood but the greater concept of the priesthood of the Christian people. Those who have the right to "reign" as priests are those who have put their life on the line for God, who in fact prefer death to unfaithfulness. The obvious reason is that they must reveal God to their people and so must be on intimate terms with God. I cannot reveal that with which I am a stranger.

The other side of priesthood is to bring the needs of the people to God. That means that I must be fully aware of what the real needs of my people are. I cannot allow myself to be part of the problem or I will have no solution to offer, or be part of the sin for then I will have no easy access to God and, besides, I will have a vested interest in not bringing the problems to God for healing. The mark of the beast is the choice to live according to worldliness, the money ethics, capitalism, the you-are-what-you-have philosophy. That obviously is what causes much of the suffering in the world. The priest must be free of that if he or she is to bring healing to the people.

When the pericope is viewed in this light, the first resurrection occurs when I put worldliness to death in my life and choose to live only for the service of God. Happy indeed am I if I achieve that because the second death, the biological death, can do me no harm. Having chosen for God, I will be with God forever. Nothing and no one can snatch that prize away from me.

Of what sense is it to call myself a priest, a servant of the Lord, unless I have achieved that freedom, to live only for God and to buy into no ego-centered worldly philosophy? Then indeed

I can reign, I can achieve the empowerment that will make me life-giving—a person of authority—to my people.

As for the thousand-year reign, perhaps more than anything else it signifies the great extent of fruitfulness that true priesthood, proper servanthood, brings me and my people. If I am truly what God has called me to be, I will do a thousand years' worth of work, of achievement, in the service of the people of God, no matter the extent of time that I spend among them.

20:7-10

The seduction of the nations began when the devil trapped the church into the games of wealth and power, then, with nationalism, put the church at the service of the state through the rise of national churches. The third step of the seduction is twofold. It surfaces as atheism, denying the very existence of God, or Satanism, choosing to fight directly against him—the Gog and Magog of this passage.

The final scene, as it is depicted here, occurs after the beast and the false prophet have been removed from the scene, a way of saying that there is no longer any subtlety to evil. It is no longer disguised as power, wealth, national pride, but appears in its undisguised horror. Those who follow Satan now follow him in full knowledge of the enormity of their action. Perhaps there is a time in the life of all sinners when the evil in their life must be confronted as evil and, if they choose to continue in it, they do so as a conscious choice against God. Damnation would not make much sense if one could be deceived into it since there would be injustice in that. Both heaven and hell must stand as a final and free decision of each human being.

The trick of the devil is to bring us so deeply into sin that, when we recognize it for what it is, we no longer have the will to live without it. To do that, he uses all the well-known slogans that represent evil as self-determination, self-gratification or freedom. Every generation gets snared by the same lies, and if there is no one to point out the traps of evil and the way out of them, many can become irrevocable slaves to hopelessness. The fire from heaven could symbolize the rage that comes with the knowledge that one has been trapped by sin and no longer sees the possibility of choosing another option because one simply lacks the will or the psychic energy to do so. By the time one recognizes a destructive habit for what it is, one is often too far gone to even want to overcome it. Many people choose to be destroyed by the habit they have acquired, be it alcohol or drugs or cigarettes or any other such thing, rather than learn to live without it.

The thought that the devil is tortured night and day forever is medieval and alien to our way of thinking, not to say repellent. Yet we might consider that, if we have trapped others into an evil that destroys them, we carry forever with us the burden of that destruction and the remorse of knowing that we have done irreparable damage. Perhaps even the devil is not beyond the possibility of remorse. What an eternal burden, what an eternal torture he must carry if he is not!

Destructive people—war criminals, mass murderers, drug dealers and such—must bear the eternal burden of the lives they have destroyed. There is no substitute for death and there is no way to reclaim a life that has gone into eternal desolation. Guilt unrepented in this life is truly the always burning fire of Gehenna.

20:11–15

As we look upon the last judgment, we enter into the deeper mystery of the book of Revelation, the final fate of humanity.

The flight of the earth and the sky reveals to us the awesomeness of the presence of God. Perhaps it also hints at the neutrality of judgment. In this context, the earth is the expectations of the world, the influence of the human condition which so often colors my behavior in this life. Judgment will not be a judgment of human expectations, of what people think of me; it will be free of all human pressures to conform. The sky is the religious tenets that I follow, my understanding of God and of morality, all the "paraphernalia of applied piety" with which I was raised and which so often stands in judgment over me in this life—in short, the often pharisaic pronouncements of established religion. Judgment will deal with my intentions—not with how well I have followed the rules but with how deeply I have wanted to be united to God and to be life-giving to other people. Judgment is a matter of who I have become rather than of what I have done or failed to do.

To be inscribed in the book of life is to have chosen life, chosen what is life-giving for myself and for others. That is the criteria of judgment—whether I have chosen life or whether I have chosen death (as is so graphically put in the book of Deuteronomy). If I have chosen life, my name is in the book of life and life is my eternal reward. If (God forbid!) I have chosen death, I receive from God that which I have chosen. If I have manipulated, dominated, used others, if I have hated, harmed, defrauded and detracted, if I have destroyed myself with bad habits and deadly choices, then I need to fear. Woe to those whose choice of death is more absolute than their choice of life! In retrospect, it is terrible and foolish to choose death, yet how many there are who appear to have done just that! Ministry is the urgent call to reverse the balance, to show life as more attractive than death, to lead people from the one to the other. It would indeed be terrible if anyone should be lost because we have failed to be good news to them. That too would be a choice of death over life. Human beings are far too precious for us to neglect any efforts to save them.

With the seventh sight, we have the final closing of the drama of the human struggle. Now what we will be looking at is the other side, the good news and the eternal triumph of holiness.

10

SEVENTH CYCLE—THE CALLS: REVELATION 21 AND 22

The book of Revelation ends with a powerful theology of church, the ideal of what we are called to be as the people of God. Our hopes, our dreams, our hungers are blessed by God and brought to eternal satisfaction.

Jesus, who has redeemed us and who has guided our journey through life, now comes forward to issue a final reminder, "I am coming very soon," to which we will respond with all our heart: "Come, Lord Jesus!" Marana tha!

PART 13—SEVENTH CYCLE:
THE CHURCH TRIUMPHANT

21:1-4

As I see it, the seventh cycle is composed of two promises by the Father—to grant us eternal consolation (21:1-4) and to make us his children (21:5-8). Following that are two works of the Holy Spirit—the building up of the church (21:9-27) and the nurturing of the church through the sacramental life (22:1-5). Finally, there are three reminders by Jesus of the imminence of the parousia— the first is the urgent call to hear the prophetic message (22:6-9), the second is a call to be ready for the Lord (22:10-15), and the third is a call to be faithful to the word (22:16-21). Thus, in its final cycle, the book of Revelation is a trinitarian message of triumph and of eager expectation ending with the impatient "Marana tha"; Come, Lord!

As we hear the first promise of triumph, God offers us a new beginning, a never-ending fulfillment. This is a beautiful image of eternal life, the home God has prepared for us, his children. Like most statements in scripture, it can be seen also on the level of our human experience. When we fully accept God as our Lord, there is for us a completely new way of looking at life; the heavens and the earth look different to us, renewed, and the sea, symbol of our human fears and insecurity, is no more. We enter into more and more perfect harmony with our world, a harmony which leads us to say with Peter: "It is good for us to be here" (Mk 9:5). It also provides us with a new understanding of religion (Jerusalem) and uncovers for us its real beauty, its real power. No longer is religion a matter of do's and don'ts, of duties and obligations. It becomes a source of joy and consolation, a freeing agent that allows us to come to God unimpeded. Religion becomes harsh and dogmatic when it is separated from the loving relationship with God which should be its center. Religion, to be truly religion, must be relational. Otherwise it can quickly become pharisaical and unbending. When religion is seen as a regulation of conduct, it tends to be harsh; when it is seen as the way to God, it becomes beautiful and truly life-giving.

God dwells with us. He will dwell with us forever. We can get away from him but we can never lose him if we seek him in sincerity and openness. How comforting that is! Relationship with God is not a matter of knowing all the right things to do but of opening our heart to love and to be loved, of coming to him with confidence and of learning from him what is right and good. Then truly he will console us and sustain us. He will drive away the tears, the sense of loss, the frustration and the pain that so often paralyze us and turn our life into a burden. With God and in his love there is no burden; there is only the realization of how deeply we are cherished and cared for. Truly, like the children that we are to him, we can rest in his arms and there feel secure forever. "If God is with us, who can be against us?" (Rom 8:31).

21:5–8

The second promise is introduced by God through seven statements that stand for the fullness of his revelation. At last the

Lord speaks clearly as he outlines for us his work in the world and what his will has brought about. Finally we can look back on our life's adventure and say: It all makes sense! This is the moment of eternal contact with God, the moment when all his children are welcomed home.

"I make all things new," God declares to us. This is the re-creation of the world on the spiritual level, the perfect level. We now enter into an eternal newness that will never become old, never grow over-familiar or boring or inadequate. Newness is the first gift we receive as we enter the presence of God. The creator welcomes us into an eternal act of creation.

"Write these matters down, for the words are trustworthy and true." The prophecy is reliable, the words of God are worthy to be preserved forever because they reveal a truth that is complete and perfect. This is the age of the Holy Spirit, the triumph of the torah of God. All that has been revealed now makes complete sense. The puzzle has been put together down to the last piece. It is our treasure and we are urged to cherish it and make it our own.

"These words are already fulfilled." With the coming of Jesus into the world, the words of scripture came to their fulfillment. We are living in the messianic era. We do not have to wait until heaven to enjoy the embrace of God; he is with us always, every day, everywhere, forever. We are already more than halfway into heaven once we have given our heart and our will over to our eternal Lord.

"I am the Alpha and the Omega, the Beginning and the End." All of history and all of reality are in God's hands. He knows what is happening, he shapes what is happening, he subjects what is happening to the accomplishment of his will. We do not need to fear; God is quite capable of handling the situation and of bringing us home. We can relax and let him take over our life completely.

"To anyone who thirsts, I will give to drink." God is refreshing us through the sacramental life of his church. The flow of his grace will never dry up. There is enough there to keep us going forever. We do not need to be afraid of using up all the benefits and of ending up wanting. No one who comes to God will ever be rejected or left unsatisfied. As Jesus said to the Samaritan woman:

"The water I give shall become a fountain within him, leaping up to provide eternal life" (Jn 4:14). Having accepted the sacramental gift of God, we now have God's life in us, and God's life is everlasting. We have been sealed with the seal of eternity.

"I will be his God and he shall be my son." This is the ultimate benefit. We are adopted into the family of God. We are his sons, his daughters, and his home is now our home. No one and nothing can ever keep us out. In receiving and living within the divine adoption, we have been assured of everlasting life.

"As for cowards . . ." Sternly, God now warns us of the kind of conduct we must stay away from. God's children do not do such things. Therefore, those who do them prove themselves not to be God's children and can make no claim to God's eternal home. The only thing left for them is the fiery pool, the eternal frustration of knowing that, through their self-centered folly, they have ruined their life, indeed missed out on their eternity.

The cosmic plan of God thus stands revealed in its fullness: what was, what is, what is to be. We have only to range ourselves firmly on the side of the victor, on the side of Christ, and we will share in the eternal triumph.

21:9-14

The first work of the Holy Spirit is the establishment of the church, the bride of Christ, gift of heaven, helpmate of the Son of God in the work of redemption. Like a diamond, the church is radiant, it is durable, it is beautiful, and it is obvious; it cannot be overlooked or ignored.

The church has twelve gates, representation of the Jewish nation from whose midst it came forth. It is the Jewish nation that has prepared the ground for this masterpiece from God, and to the Jewish nation belongs the honor of presenting it to the world. That the church and the synagogue should have parted company does not change the fact that they share a common ancestry and that it is through the synagogue that the church has made its entrance into the world.

The gates face all four directions, an indication that the church is open to all the nations of the earth. No one can be kept out because of race, ethnic differences or culture. The church belongs to the world and can never close its doors on the world.

The church has twelve foundation stones. It is founded on the witness and the proclamation of the twelve apostles of Jesus; hence it is based on the teachings of Jesus himself. It is he who has given the world this new and deeper concept of religion that we call Christianity.

Gift to the world from the synagogue, founded on the teachings of the apostles of Jesus, the church remains the cooperative achievement of Jews and Christians and both deserve credit for its transforming work in the world.

21:15-21

The perfect squareness of the city symbolizes its orderliness. In the city of God, the church, there is no chaos. Everything fits perfectly: dogmas, rituals, ethics. It is a perfect whole. It is also immense; fifteen hundred miles long, wide and high. Hence there is plenty of room for anyone who chooses to come in. It will never be completely full.

The image of the precious stones is as meaningful as it is beautiful. The number twelve hints that the stones are related to the believers and possibly represent the variety of talents that God has given to his people, all of which are precious. We are a gifted people, each in our own way, and we ought never to depreciate our giftedness.

One could go a long way in reflecting on the imagery of this passage, some of which has been lost to us because we are no longer sure of the meaning for the first-century Christians of the various stones mentioned. The number one hundred and forty-four in relation to the wall is, of course, twelve times twelve and so is related to the Christians—not just the Christians of the seer's time but all the Christians of all the centuries of the church. It is they who defend and protect the structure of the church. Each generation is called to polish its beauty and lead it to ongoing purification so it will remain secure in the love of God.

In a mixed metaphor, the gold of the streets is transparent. The church is not a secret society, it is a city set on a hill, and all its activities must be transparent to the world. Things done in secret have no part in the church. All the actions of the people of God must be able to stand the challenge of the world. It is in accepting criticism that we grow, not in avoiding it through secrecy.

21:22-27

This last paragraph is rich in imagery as it presents the church's relationship with God and the requirements for membership in it. There is no temple because God is always a free agent; we can never imprison him in a building or even in one specific way of worshiping. We are also reminded that there is no need for a temple since we, the believing people, are the temple of God, the only temple in which he resides, by his choice rather than by ours.

God is the sun because his presence dissipates all the darkness, all the errors that could otherwise creep into the church. The Lamb is the moon that shines in darkness, that allows us to experience hope even in the night of persecution from the world. No persecution can overcome the church because Jesus is in its midst, as solidly on our side as the moon is solidly in the heavens.

The gates of the city of God are never shut. There is never a time when we can close the door of the church to those who wish to enter. The opportunity to be one with us must never be denied anyone who sincerely wants to join us. The church is not an in-group, a private club; everyone in the world has a right to be part of it. More important still, perhaps, the church must acknowledge that everyone who comes in enters with riches and wealth. The newcomers also have something to offer to enrich the church— customs, ethical values, styles of worship. Too often we feel that newcomers should abandon all of their past ways and just do things as we do. This prophecy militates against such an attitude. The wealth of all the nations can enrich the church and none should be arbitrarily rejected because we do not want to expend the energy or take the risk to make it fit. How many converted nations have been hurt because, in our narrowness of vision, we have failed to heed this prophecy of the book of Revelation!

Having looked at who can come in, we now look at the conditions that the newcomers need to fulfill if they would be part of us. There is an ethical value system that the church cannot abandon just so people will get in more easily. We are a counter-sign to the world, a proof that there are other values besides selfishness, pride, possessions and all that the world preaches with such enticing insistence. Those who would follow those ethics of worldliness really have no part in the church; they don't fit in. Nothing must be sacrificed for the sake of mere numbers.

Liars cannot come in. Liars are those people who join the church for the wrong reasons. Prestige, profit, public opinion, anything that is not concerned with a right relationship with God and with other people is a lie against what must be the real purpose for joining the church. There have been too many liars in the church. It is time, perhaps, that they should be challenged to grow or go.

Those who do detestable acts are those who join the church without the determination to amend their lives. If one does not wish to follow the ethical teachings of the church, that person has no place in the church. The purity of the faith must not be compromised for the sake of worldly values or comforts. There are demands on the Christians to live according to the ways of righteousness. Those who have no concern for righteousness do not belong; they are the wolves among the sheep.

The only people who belong in the city of God, then, are those whose name is written in the book of the living which is in the possession of the Lamb, those who have chosen to live according to the ethics of salvation and whose hearts are firmly directed toward a loving relationship with God and neighbor. What a challenge there is in this for us who, sometimes perhaps too lightly, choose to call ourselves Christians!

22:1-5

The second work of the Holy Spirit is the sacramental life of the church which is depicted here as a river of life-giving water besides which the trees of life (the sacraments) grow. The tree-sacraments bear fruit twelve times a year, that is, continually. This is also a reminder that the fruits are for the people of God, those in good standing in the church, represented by the number twelve. Hence we have a double meaning intended—of continuity and of Christianity. The tree also has leaves for medicine—the sacraments of healing (baptism, reconciliation, anointing of the sick). The healing is "for the nations," those who are not fully a part of the church through either a lack of conversion or a fall from grace.

As for the Christians, those who stand in the presence of God because they have chosen holiness, they have no need of light except for the light of God. The only truth that matters to them is the truth revealed by God. It is not from nature (the sun) or from human science (the lamp) that we get our true knowledge but from God alone. If we possess this all-important truth, then we do indeed reign with God, that is, share in his divine life.

22:6–9

The first call of Jesus, the first "I am coming soon," invites us—indeed warns us—to take the prophecy of Revelation seriously. It includes the fifth beatitude which relates to our ability to listen well. The better we can listen to God, the more profoundly we will be blessed by him and the more fruitful our life will be. To be a contemplative is a necessary element of anyone's prayer life; otherwise, we might miss too much that is of vital importance to us and to our world.

There is an urgency in this final chapter of Revelation, a sense that the end is coming soon, that the drama is heading toward its fulfillment. There is, especially, an assurance that the message is trustworthy, that we can stake our lives on it, that it is in fact what God is calling us to. We are to live in integrity and not be swallowed up by the concerns, the greeds, the sins of this world (the mark of the beast). Rather, we need to lift our thoughts and hearts toward the greater truth of God's kingdom, to live with integrity in the service of the Lord Jesus, and to be messengers of his good news (the mark of the Lamb).

The heavenly messenger has come to tell us that there is more to life than life. But I think he tells us something more—that we are slated someday to be on a par with him, to be messengers of

God into the world of his creation at another time and perhaps another place. "I am a fellow servant with you." We are called to a dignity, a cosmic task that we have not yet even begun to understand.

22:10-11

The first call of Jesus ends with a reflection that exemplifies the balance always present in the book. There are four kinds of people listed, two negatives and two positives. The passage starts with a warning to the seer not to seal the message, that is, not to keep it to himself but to share it with others. The revelations of God in our life are not only for us but are meant to be shared with others so that all may benefit from the insight of each person. There are things that have to be said for the good of all and, if we fail to say them, we may be using more timidity than discretion. When people's welfare and happiness depend on our speaking, we cannot simply remain silent.

The time is near, we are told. The time is always near; a lifetime is very short and an eternity is very long. Putting off conversion can be a dangerous thing; we could find ourselves with too little time or too little energy to do it well and end up with the eternal regret of not having sufficiently cooperated, of having in fact missed the boat.

The two negative types listed here are the wicked, those who hurt others, who are guilty of injustice, and the depraved, those who hurt their own integrity, who are guilty of unholy living. The two positives are the virtuous, those who do good deeds, who live in justice, and the holy, those whose personal lives reflect the integrity that God calls us to. Until the end of time, the two contrasting types will be there. We will always have the opportunity to make a free choice in our life; therefore both negatives and positives must always be possible.

22:12-16

As the drama of humanity comes to its conclusion, we are given another image of the cosmic Christ who is behind the drama and leads it to fulfillment. The section begins with a warning ("I am coming soon") and a promise ("I bring the reward"). Then three cosmic titles follow. Jesus is Alpha and Omega, the fullness of reality. He is the First and the Last, the fullness of human accomplishment. He is the Beginning and the End, the fullness of human history. A further word on the second title: the First and the Last implies that Jesus is part of every human being created by God; he is in all of us and thus renders all of us heirs of heaven if we also will be part of him.

Verse 14 gives us the seventh beatitude. It is good indeed to belong to the following of the Lord, to be cleansed by his blood and eat of the tree of life (his eucharistic life) and to be part of his church (the holy city). One is either a friend of the Lord or a sinner.

What follows the beatitude is a list of sins—six only because there is no perfection in sin. They are listed two by two, a reminder that sin begets more sin and that, when we start down that slippery slope, we quickly acquire more and more bad habits. All the sins are in some way negations of truth and life.

Two more titles of Jesus follow. He is the Root and Offspring of David, the fulfillment of prophecy. The reality of Jesus is contained in all of past history which has led inevitably to him. He is the Morning Star, the new beginning, the hope of the future. He is all that was and all that is to be. He is rooted in earth and he reaches out to the heavens. We stand in awe before this wondrous reality of the Lord and his centrality in our life. We either live with him or we do not live at all; we remain the living dead.

22:17

The chiastic structure of the book of Revelation ends with the third call, the seventh part of the cycle of the church. Three invitations to life are presented to us. The Spirit invites us to share in the gifts of the church and the promise of eternal life. Echoing his invitation, the church (the bride) also calls us to come, to take part in its gifts and benefits. Then all of us who have received the invitation are urged to pass it on, to bring others to the life-giving water of the church which is Christ. He who animates the church, the church itself, and all who are animated by the church call out the invitation to be the people of the Lord. We are an open society in which there is room for all who are thirsting for God and who are willing to pay the price for possessing him.

22:18–19

Two warnings are placed here, at the end of the book. We have heard the testimony of the Lord. If we add to it any purely human inventions (false theologies, heresies) or if we take away (deny) any part of the Lord's message (again a matter of heresy), then we do not belong to the following of the Lord. His word is to be accepted in its entirety, not tacked on to other teachings and not edited for the sake of personal comfort. It is a hard saying but it brings us to eternal life. To alter it would be to become guilty of a lie and thus to wander into the camp of the enemy who mouths lies as though they were pious truths, thus incurring the plagues which are the inevitable results of evil living.

22:20–21

There is a longing and a wistfulness at the end of this great book. Jesus himself is longing to come to us, impatient to complete the tremendous task he has come to earth to inaugurate. A responding longing is ours as we contemplate all that has been promised us, all that we stand to gain by his coming. Indeed, what a wonderful day will be the day of our death! Then we will never more sin or go astray or hear any lying voices or be confused or hurt or frustrated. Come! Yes, come, Lord Jesus! There will be no greater day in our life than the day you take us home.

Amen.

11

FINAL REFLECTIONS

CONCLUSION

Perhaps one of the most important things to remember about the book of Revelation is that it is an examination of conscience for Christians, a proper tool for discernment in our day to day decisions as we strive to live the calling that we have embraced at baptism. The book is not—and this must be emphasized—a tool for judging the world or for deciding who are the good people and who are the bad people. In my estimation it has been used for that purpose far too often in the past.

One of my experiences of this spirit of judgmentality for which Revelation can be used concerns a native American lady who came to me some years ago. She was quite upset by something she had been told in a Fundamentalist class on Revelation, namely that all her ancestors were in hell because they had not professed Jesus as Lord, something they could not very well have done since they did not know him. That is what I mean by improper use of Revelation. When scripture is used as a weapon for judgment rather than as a tool for discernment, I have no doubt that it is being used improperly.

We need to reflect on our society because we are part of it and we will be shaped and influenced by it knowingly or unknowingly. However, if our reflection remains on society and never comes down to personal appraisal, we will not benefit fully from the reflection. I am part of my society and my society is part of me. As we are individually, so are we as a nation. To divorce myself from the problems around me is an attitude that is both elitist and sterile. Knowing the sins of others is of little benefit to me unless it helps me to discover my own sinfulness. It is neither wise nor just to solve other people's problems if I remain blind to my own.

Once I become aware that Revelation is a tool for personal discernment rather than a call to social action, I can begin to understand it better and especially to understand why it says so little about works of charity and proclamation of the Lord. These things can only be done fruitfully if I have challenged the attitudes that I find within myself. Otherwise I may easily slip from proper ministry to judgmentality and do-gooder activities that may be little better than enabling. Revelation helps me to look at myself so that I can better and more fruitfully enter the realm of ministry.

In our reflection on the book, we first became acquainted with its divine and human authors and, above all, with what it takes for us to be proper revealers of the divine will. Authorship, in scripture, has a much broader interpretation than we are used to. The author may be the actual writer (Luke the evangelist), the secretary who receives and often reshapes the message (the epistles of Paul) or simply the one whose preaching has inspired the writing of the book (possibly the gospels of Matthew and of John). What we must remember, when we read Revelation, is that its author, in scriptural protocol, is not John but Jesus himself. To read the book in any other spirit is, at least partly, to miss the point.

Having established authorship as it is understood in Revelation, we entered the cyclic movement of the book by first looking at our life from the point of view of being a church community. To understand my own attitudes toward the church, I need to study the attitudes of the community that surrounds me and to reflect on how that attitude may be influencing my own. The warning to the churches is a warning to look at the attitudes that permeate my immediate faith-community—parish, diocese, religious order, lay association, etc.—and to challenge those attitudes that do not reflect properly the message of Jesus. We are responsible for the proclamation of the word and we proclaim it far more with our life than with our words. We *are* the words of Jesus; we do not simply proclaim those words.

To understand my attitudes properly, I need to look not just around me but also within myself. What are the fears, the hurts, the sufferings that have accumulated within me over the years? Everything I see and hear as well as everything I say is going to be colored by those inner feelings that I carry. My emotions are the filters of my understanding. If I am not properly attuned to those emotions, I will tend to act in an irrational fashion that will not communicate so much the message of my Lord as my own personal woundedness. We can readily see the results when, for instance, someone enters the ministry of justice and peace because of personal anger. Sadly, such people are likely to show little justice and to bring about little peace until they have dealt with their own inner anger.

Once I have looked at my pain, I still need to look at what has caused that pain and that brings us to the third cycle, the cycle of sin. The deepest pain within each of us is caused not by natural calamity (handicaps, sickness, accidents) but by sin, the sins we have committed (our own foolish mistakes) and, even more profoundly, the sins others have committed against us (injustices, manipulation, neglect, abuse, etc.). If I do not understand this connection between pain and sin, I will not know how to exorcise the demons within that control my behavior and my reactions toward other people. The deepest hurts of our life are like the demon in Mark 9:17—they are mute, they cannot reveal themselves to us, we have to search them out with prayer and fasting (Mt 17:21).

As the author brings us deeper into our self-examination, we come to the next problem: If there is sin in the world, why is it there? What has brought it about? How does it attack us and what can we do to counter the attack? This is the apex of the chiasmus, the central message, the inner core of the revelation. We are caught up in an ideological struggle between good and evil that has been with us since the dawn of history, since the adam (the human being) was fashioned from the clay of the earth.

This cosmic struggle that Revelation presents to us is not just out there in society; it is also in the very core of each and every one of us. It is not just the world's struggle, it is my struggle, and I must resolve it first within my own being if I can hope to bring a viable solution for it to the world around me. This is why a judgmental attitude is so insidious. When I begin to point fingers, when I divorce myself from the problem, I am no longer in a position to bring to it a successful solution. As I am fond of saying to the people who come to me for direction, the only rascal I can look at constructively is the rascal within my own bosom.

After this profound look at the ideological struggle, Revelation takes another perspective and now begins to look at how my sinfulness can become the burden not just of the people around me but of nature itself. The cycle of the bowls forces me to look at the results of my sins, at the havoc that I may be wreaking around me. There is no sin that is completely a private sin. It will always hurt more than myself. By my actions, by my attitude, even by my neglect, I will pass on some hurt to others—indeed to nature itself—through every sin that I surrender myself to. The greatest fallacy of our modern era is the oft-repeated statement: "It's my life and I have the right to live it the way I want to." Those who buy into that lie can very quickly become the spoilers of life. We are social beings whether we like it or not. What we do will have an impact on others, on nature, on the future generations. We can do tremendous good in our world and we can do tremendous harm. That is how God, the eternally perfect community, has created us. That is what it means to be his image and likeness. We have an obligation to our world that we can never elude, no matter how much we might want to.

Since this communal aspect cannot be ignored, we need to know what to do about the harm perpetrated by sin and selfishness. This brings us to the sixth cycle in which is played out the proper and successful challenging of the social situation that we live in. How do we, the people of God, deal with the harm that is done by ambition, greed, selfishness and sin in our world? To know the problem is of little value unless we are also given the possibility of a solution.

The final cycle returns us to the church community where we began our scrutiny. What are the hopes on which we base our life? What are the values we are striving to present to the world? And, above all, what is the criterion for being a fruitful member of the church? The book, cyclic to the end, brings us back to the beginning, to the presence of Jesus challenging us from within and calling us to live life with holiness and to pass on the message of hope and of warning to others. We cannot "seal up the prophetic word" (Rev 22:10). Once we have made it our own, we must pass it on lest we incur the condemnation that is found in the book of Ezekiel: "If I say to the wicked man, 'You shall surely die,' and you do not warn him or speak out to dissuade him from his wicked conduct so that he may live, that wicked man shall die for his sin, but I will hold you responsible for his death" (Ez 3:18). This is indeed a sobering thought and a great incentive to look at the abyss within and to dissipate the smoke of rationalization that can hide from us our great need for ongoing repentance (Rev 9:2).

12

SUGGESTIONS FOR FURTHER READING

Beasley-Murray, G. R., "Revelation," *The New Century Bible Commentary*. Eerdmans, 1981.

Collins, Adela Yarbro, *The Apocalypse,* ("New Testament Message" 22). Michael Glazier, 1979.

Harrington, Wilfrid, *Understanding the Apocalypse.* Corpus, 1969.

Kealy, Sean P., *The Apocalypse of John* ("Message of Biblical Spirituality" 15), Michael Glazier.

Perkins, Pheme, "The Book of Revelation," *Collegeville Bible Commentary* 11). The Liturgical Press, 1983.